REPRESENTING THE FASHION OF OUR NINETEENTH CENTURY CHEROKEE ANCESTOR

Lara Neel and Lisa Neel

REPRESENTING THE FASHION OF OUR NINETEENTH CENTURY CHEROKEE ANCESTOR

Culture Not Costume

The Fashion and Personal Style Studies Collection

Collection Editor
Joseph H. Hancock II

For all of the mouths that lay with stories buried within them. We are listening.

First published in 2025 by Lived Places Publishing

All rights reserved. No part of this publication may be reproduced, stored in a retrieval system, or transmitted in any form or by any means, electronic, mechanical, photocopying, recording, or otherwise, without prior permission in writing from the publisher.

No part of this book may be used or reproduced in any manner for the purpose of training artificial intelligence technologies or systems. In accordance with Article 4(3) of the Digital Single Market Directive 2019/790, Lived Places Publishing expressly reserves this work from the text and data mining exception.

The author and editor have made every effort to ensure the accuracy of information contained in this publication but assume no responsibility for any errors, inaccuracies, inconsistencies, and omissions. Likewise, every effort has been made to contact copyright holders. If any copyright material has been reproduced unwittingly and without permission, the publisher will gladly receive information enabling them to rectify any error or omission in subsequent editions.

Copyright © 2025 Lived Places Publishing

British Library Cataloguing in Publication Data
A CIP record for this book is available from the British Library.

ISBN: 9781916985391 (pbk)
ISBN: 9781916985414 (ePDF)
ISBN: 9781916985407 (ePUB)

The right of Lara Neel and Lisa Neel to be identified as the Authors of this work has been asserted by them in accordance with the Copyright, Design and Patents Act 1988.

Cover design by Fiachra McCarthy
Book design by Rachel Trolove of Twin Trail Design
Typeset by Newgen Publishing, UK

Lived Places Publishing
P.O. Box 1845
47 Echo Avenue
Miller Place, NY 11764

www.livedplacespublishing.com

Acknowledgements

We'd like to thank our families, especially our spouses and children (both human and fur-bearing), who let us make the space in our lives to write, edit, read, and film.

We give special thanks to all the authors of our sources, and to the networks of people who preserved their words.

Abstract

Drawing directly from their own family's history, authors Lara Neel and Lisa Neel critique the misrepresentation and erasure of Native American history. Exploring the intersection of womanhood and identity in the Cherokee Nation, this work follows Lara and Lisa's investigation into the life of their murdered maternal ancestor. By using academic research to unravel deeply ingrained historical contradictions and construct a woman-focused Native American history, they make a case for the importance of perspective and representation in the modern living history community and the lasting effects misrepresentation has on one of the largest Native American tribes in the United States.

Keywords

History; Native American; Cherokee; indigenous; gender; womanhood; multiracial lineage; sociology; representation; lived experience; living history community; Civil War

Contents

Note on language		viii
Content warning		x
Introduction		xi
Learning objectives		xiii
Chapter 1	"Tell them who you are"	1
Chapter 2	Cherokee culture in the nineteenth century: Negotiation, self-presentation, and calico dresses	27
Chapter 3	Why it matters: Investigating the archives and embracing all legal Cherokees	81
Chapter 4	How we "dressed" Polly to bring her into the picture	103
Chapter 5	Living anti-racist history and opening the archives	157
Chapter 6	Honoring Polly Beck	181
Recommended discussion questions		184
Notes		185
References		187
Recommended further reading		204
Index		205

Note on language

English is an elastic, expansive language. Words and phrases take on new meanings, shed nuance, and can grow teeth and pointy elbows over time. In taking up the work of researching, then writing about Cherokee cultural change in the nineteenth century, we joined a long tradition of Cherokee and non-Cherokee voices.

In this book, we quote heavily from primary sources. Some of these sources use slurs or terms that have become slurs in the time since their original publication. We have chosen to redact slurs, using person-centered wording when such alternatives exist in current common use. When these do not exist, we simply say, "slur." In case your academic work requires the uncensored language, you should easily be able to find it yourself through our careful documentation of references.

We have avoided using the term slave, preferring the person-centered terms enslaved person or bondsperson. We left references to "freedmen" intact.

The term Indian is not *always* a slur, but it is loaded. We have generally preferred the terms Native American or Native only when discussing citizens of tribal nations. When possible, we use the person's tribal citizenship as their primary identifier.

We struggled with the best way to refer to English and European colonists and then, later, United States citizens primarily descended from European people. White people, Aliens, Caucasians, Euro-Americans, Anglo-Americans, and colonizers were all unsatisfactory, although we have retained them when found in quoted sources. The Cherokee language has a word for "outsider" that loses nuance in a text otherwise written in English. We settled on "English Colonists" before 1775 and "White Americans" after 1775. While not all white-coded, non-Native colonists originated from England itself; they immigrated or emigrated to the areas surrounding the Cherokee Nation under the jurisdiction of English law and treaties.

Our time period is cut through by the United States Civil War. When we discuss the armed participants in this conflict, we use the terms "Union Army" and the "Confederate States Army" even when the fighters were not officially wearing uniforms.

Marriages, admiration for specific mentors, or significant life events could all lead to a Cherokee changing their name. To reduce confusion, we use the "nee" structure when possible to link people to their natal family name throughout their lifetimes.

Some Cherokee words used in this text

We don't speak Cherokee fluently, or very well at all, to be honest. Our maternal grandfather, L.C. Neel, pretended not to speak Cherokee at all, although he occasionally muttered phrases under his breath.

We're biased, but Cherokee really is a beautiful language, focused on action and relationships. If you want to hear the word we ended up using, you should visit the Cherokee Nation YouTube channel.

Se-qua (https://www.youtube.com/watch?v=0Sq9EvQhC2g)

Content warning

This book contains explicit references to, and descriptions of, situations that may cause distress. This includes references to and descriptions of:

- Violent assault (including murder)
- Chattel slavery
- Racial discrimination
- Micro-aggressions
- Colonization

Please be aware that references to potentially distressing topics occur **frequently** and **throughout** the book.

Introduction

Talking Leaves and oral tradition

We both live in houses that practically groan with books. Generally, we have a lifelong love of reading that fits into one of the modern stereotypes about Cherokees: our early and aggressive adaptation to reading in English was reportedly thorough and intense, and we still deeply revere Sequoyah and his work to bring writing and reading to the Cherokee language.

This book is our dual autobiography of how we developed a reframed and secondhand biography of Polly Beck. She's still a mystery to us in many ways. This work is relatively heavy on references and formal documentation for people who are not the primary subject. We did that intentionally. The oral tradition has an important place in how we tell our stories, but we wanted to rely on the durability and reach of written words to support our suppositions and interpretations.

As part of our antiracist values, we strive to educate ourselves without burdening others when learning about experiences we don't share. We hope this book sparks curiosity about the Cherokee Nation and invites reflection about the United States' ongoing relationship with tribes, other nations, and all the inhabitants and citizens of this country (Fig. 1).

Fig. 1 Lara and Lisa in a mirror, November 2024. Photo by Lara Neel.

Learning objectives

1. Readers should learn how to use historic primary documents and secondary sources to explore parts of history that have not been directly written. For example, women's history is often overlooked, but there's still a lot to see if you learn to read between the lines.
2. It is an unfortunate fact that non-white people often upheld the systems built upon white supremacy. Chattel slavery is among them. The Cherokee enslavement of African-descended people is one example of non-white groups doing just that.
3. Modern Native American identity is impossible to understand without attempting to learn at least some of the history of how it is defined by Native Americans and federal government entities alike. This work may serve as a case study of that history.

1
"Tell them who you are"

> "The indigenous tragedy of a people surviving genocide, orphaned, displaced, and largely deculturated in their own homeland, is *the* tragedy of this country, affecting everyone far more than most of us realize. It lies buried, invisible beneath the histories (plural, multidimensional) taught in schools and universities, beneath the history (singular, one-dimensional) officially assumed, even beneath the stories of lives lived and experienced individually, locally. It is the bump under the carpet of colonialism, the nightmare at the edge of communal sleep" (Lippard, 1992, p. 19).

On February 13, 1872, our grandfather's great-grandmother was murdered. The shooting was either part of a longer feud, an accident, or a little of both. We had always heard of her as a tragic figure. Her killer ultimately went unpunished, except possibly by his conscience.

We have no images of her. When she's even mentioned in sources, many of them depict the Beck Hildebrand Mill as a stand-in for her and our family, often right across the page from a late-in-life photograph of her killer (Conley. 2005, pp. 126–127).

Even her name was disputed among her relatives less than 50 years after her death. A search for her mother's name in the series: "Eastern Cherokee Applications, August 29, 1906–May 26, 1909" held at the United States National Archives yields distant cousins, nieces, nephews, and direct descendants that list Polly among her siblings as:

Mary or Polly Hildebrand (Eastern Cherokee Applications, Application No. 859, p. 5)

Mary Beck (Eastern Cherokee Applications, Application No. 868, p. 5 and, Eastern Cherokee Applications, Application No. 867, p. 5)

Polly Kesterson (Eastern Cherokee Applications, Application No. 1335, p. 5)

Polly Kesterson nee Beck (Eastern Cherokee Applications, Application No. 4690, p. 5)

Polly Beck Hilderbrand (Eastern Cherokee Applications, Application No. 2157, p. 7)

Pauline Kesterson (Eastern Cherokee Applications, Application No. 10928, p. 5)

Everyone that gives a death date gives the same, uncommonly specific one: February 13, 1872.

We don't know where she is buried. Family oral history reports that her remains are in the Joseph Beck Family Cemetery, near the town of Flint, Oklahoma, in Delaware County. But she has no stone or marker. The only large memorial in that cemetery belongs to her brother Joseph Beck, Sr. and his wife, Cynthia Downing Beck, both dead about a decade before Polly.

Emmet Starr's foundational work: "History of the Cherokee Indians and Their Legends and Folk Lore" (pp. 306–307) lists her as "Pauline Beck," child of Susannah Buffington and Jeffrey Beck. He notes she was married to a succession of four husbands: Aaron Downing, James Crittenden, Stephen Hildebrand, and James Kesterson.

We've always known her as Polly Beck. As children, little bits of the story would be revealed to us, often casually and sparked by "Old West" themes in television (TV) shows or movies. "We have ancestors who died in gun fights back before statehood…"

In the late 2010s, Lara got interested in her story and started researching her actual life, not just her regionally famous death. In 2023, we decided to start putting together a full set of clothes to depict her as part of a larger craftivism project. It was a new part of dress history for both of us and an interesting way to virtually spend more time together. We knew the time period would require some navigation of the ethics and milieu of creating and wearing historically based garments of the nineteenth century in Indian Territory.

Researching Polly Beck led us places we didn't expect to go. We thought we'd spend a few months sewing petticoats, sourcing textiles, and getting more comfortable with horizontal buttonholes on our dress bodices. Answering the question, "What would Polly have worn in her lifetime?" led us to gather evidence that forced us to question many of our own assumptions about our family and the larger Cherokee Nation.

These questions were:

- How did our ancestors see themselves and seek to represent themselves to the world?
- What did Cherokee women wear in the nineteenth century?
- Did Cherokee families have access to current news, including fashion's changes?
- As modern antiracists, are we helpless to reduce the harm of chattel slavery's legacy?

There are a lot of things we don't know about Polly's life and death. Sources focus on the aftermath and do not tell us, for example, whether the survivors followed the tradition reported by the Kilpatricks.

> "when someone died during the night, it was traditional to tack a notice to the church door at sunrise and to ring the church bell so the community might inform itself of the name of the deceased and the particulars of the forthcoming funeral…the notice was written in the [Cherokee] syllabary, often in elaborations of the symbols, and sometimes scenes from the deceased person's life were drawn on the paper" (Parins, 2003, p. 108).

We had to start with a brief review of the primary and secondary sources mentioning what happened at the Hildebrand Mill and the Goingsnake schoolhouse in 1872. While much ink has been spilled on this topic of the shootout, very little covers Polly's life itself. We'll start with the end of her life's story and explain how we worked backward.

One of the most explicit descriptions of Polly's status as something other than a victim is included in an application for designation

Fig. 1.1 The Hildebrand Mill. Public Domain National Archives and Records Administration record, Oklahoma SP Hildebrand Mill (National Archives Identifier: 86511065) The rebuilt mill as it stood in the twentieth century.

as a Historic Place for the building of the mill itself. Written in 1972, almost exactly 100 years after her death, the author notes:

"Sometime before the Civil War Stephen Hildebrand married Pauline ("Aunt Polly") Beck. This not only brought the Beck family name into the history of Hildebrand Mill, but also laid the foundation for controversy and bloody strife that soon surrounded it" (National Archives Catalog, 1972, p. 5).

While this document focuses on the salacious details of firearm violence and the mill itself as a piece of important infrastructure, it also provides us with important perspectives on Polly's ownership and management of it. This is one of the only references that goes beyond framing her as the wife or widow of a series of men. In fact, the author tried to untangle which Hildebrand was "the" Hildebrand based on Stephen Hildebrand's marriage to Polly, not the other way around:

> "Shortly after completing the mill Towers sold it to Stephen Hildebrand. Here again confusion exists, as some written records refer to the new owner as Peter Hildebrand, an uncle of Stephen and a man of means in Tennessee before coming to Indian Territory where, according to
> Starr, he operated 'a saw, turning and grist mill.' He died Dec. 11, 1861. However, Stephen was the son of Michael, a brother of Peter. Michael was also [an enslaver] of substance in Tennessee, and the owner of two mills, so Stephen grew up with a strong milling background. His presumed ownership is based on his marriage to Pauline Beck" (National Archives Catalog, 1972, p. 5).

In contrast, the reports submitted to the United States Congress by the President of the United States, Ulysses S. Grant, mere weeks after the "Difficulties in Cherokee Country" include a number of eyewitness and secondhand accounts who contradict and seek to indict each other for the violence. Even as close to the events as April 29, 1872, the absolute truth and agency of the actors was hidden, managed, and spun. White American sources, written in English, began at a potential disadvantage, which was compounded by sensationalism. Many Cherokee trials in this era were held in Cherokee and later translated in English. "Testimony was often given in the native language, and because of the lack of an accurate, rapid system of recording, the actual court proceedings were not recorded" (Parins, 2003, p. 124). A shorthand in Cherokee wasn't available until 1891 (Parins, 2003, p. 125).

> "While the counsel for the defense was reviewing the evidence, the court was interrupted
> by the approach of several deputy United States marshals, with an advance posse armed with guns, some of which posse were near relatives of the deceased, and were known to be determined on the conviction or rescue of the prisoner, ordered the sheriff to recede, and leveled a gun at the prisoner's body, who, while attempting to ward it aside, received the discharge in his leg, and at the same time the contents of another gun was discharged into the body of the prisoner's counsel…the result was…the killing of ten or eleven, and the wounding of several others" (H.R. Exec. No. 287, 42nd Cong., 2nd Sess., 1872, p. 3).

Writing in 1873 (McLoughlin, 1993, p. 310), Cherokee petitioners to the United States, James M. Bell and Sut Beck (who participated in the Federal posse himself) included the murder trial in a list of injustices and examples of lawlessness while seeking to encourage their fellow Cherokee citizens to support the division and allotment of Cherokee lands in Indian Territory:

> "Our laws are trampled upon. The honest and quiet citizens are the mercy of desperadoes and outlaws… Look at the case of the murder of Hicks, and the train of violence, bloodshed, and arson that followed it; the murder of Mrs. Chesterson by Proctor…The trials in all these cases, and dozens more we might mention, were so many farces: a miserable compromise between crime and the law; between riot and order; between a set of murderous desperadoes and the officers of the law. Is this carnival of crime and blood to continue, without protest, because forsooth the delegation don't choose to expose and denounce it?" (Bell and Beck, n.d., verso)

Polly's story is easily lost in the deep shadow of the events that followed her death. One of the main reasons we wanted to pursue details about her is that historians and even contemporary accounts sometimes neglect to even mention her name or provide any details about her. The following oral history, from a man who was 14 years old at the time, is one of the more detailed reports of her death, mentioning her own actions. It is, partially, a second-hand account, but it may be closer to the truth than nearly any newspaper tale, as public interest in the story didn't start up until after Zeke Proctor's fateful day in court.

The Widow Hilderbrand[1]

"On a picturesque little stream called Flint Creek stands a historical mill called the Hilderbrand Mill, where once lived the Widow Hilderbrand. However, at the time of this story, Mrs. Hilderbrand had married again, this time to a man named Jim Kesterman.[2] It was at this mill that a great tragedy occurred which later developed into what is known as the 'Proctor Fight.'... 'Aunt Polly,' as she was usually called by those who knew her best, was a... [mixed race] ...Cherokee Indian, and Kesterman was a white man. They were considered law-abiding citizens. White Sut Beck, Black Sut Beck, and Sam and Bill Beck also were [mixed race] Cherokees and nephews of Mrs. Kesterman.

During the Civil War the Becks and Zeke Proctor served in the army but under different flags. Proctor served in the Federal Army and the Becks in the Confederate Army. Nevertheless, they were good friends until the trouble started which I will write about...[original ellipses]

It was sometime during the month of February 1872, that Proctor and Kesterman began having trouble over some stock. Proctor lived about ten miles from the Hilderbrand Mill. One morning he saddled his horse and rode over to the mill to talk the matter over with Kesterman. He bade them the time of day, and the talk drifted to the trouble about the stock. Finally, they got into a heated argument, and it would be impossible to tell all that was said, as I am only telling it as I heard it told. Proctor, seeing Kesterman reach for his gun, drew his gun and fired. Mrs. Kesterman, thinking that she might save her husband, ran in between the two men and the bullet intended for Kesterman hit her, killing her instantly. Kesterman then ran up the steps to a second story of the mill. Proctor fired two more shots at his retreating figure, shooting two holes in the latter's coat. Proctor then mounted his horse and rode away.

Arriving at his home, he told what he had done. He then sent a man to tell Jack Wright, who was sheriff of Goingsnake District, of the affair. Jack Wright lived about five miles east of Baron Creek Station. When the man delivered the Proctor message to him, he went over and arrested Proctor, placed a guard over him, and reported the case to the prosecuting attorney.

Cornick Sixkiller was appointed special judge to try the case. On April 1872, the case was called. Proctor was arraigned for trial, and, while the lawyers were arguing, up rode a posse of men headed by Deputy U. S. Marshal Owens accompanied by White Sut Beck, a nephew of Mrs. Kesterman, the other Becks already being there on the ground and heavily armed back in a grove where stood the little log school house that is known as the Whitmire School, which was being used on this special occasion as a court house…[original ellipses]

White Sut Beck seemed to be leading the marshal's forces and with his crowd made for the court house. Sut Beck leveled a double-barreled shotgun on Zeke Proctor. Then Johnson Proctor, a brother to Zeke, grabbed the gun and received the full charge of shot in his breast, the other load striking Zeke in the knee. The battle was then on, and it would be impossible to describe the horrible and bloody scene that followed. The firing of guns got so rapid that the bullets rained like hail in every direction. For a moment it seemed like a duel to the death on both sides, but finally the posse fled before the bullets from Proctor's side.

When the smoke of the battle had cleared away, the ground in front of the little log school house was covered with the dead and the wounded. Proctor had his men, what was left of them, and stood victor over the scene. Nine men were killed and two were mortally wounded.

About an hour later, my mother who was a widow had us boys to hitch a span of mules to the wagon, drive to the scene of the battle, and with the assistance of Proctor and his men, the dead and wounded were loaded into the wagon and taken to our house. The wounded were carried into the house, which was converted into a temporary hospital, until the relatives came and took them away. The nine dead men were laid on our big porch… [original ellipses]

My eldest brother, Steve Whitmire, and the school teacher, whose name was Mack, saw the whole affair from start to finish. The teacher had dismissed school, and he and my brother had stayed at court.

When the excitement had somewhat died down, the sheriff took Proctor over to the old Scraper home where he was guarded until the next day. He was then tried by a jury of twelve men and found 'not guilty.'

After the events above described, society was thrown into a turmoil from which it took a long time to recover and to discuss the terrible battle, which was destined to leave a lasting impression on the minds of so many people" (Perdue, 1993, pp. 23–25).

This turmoil led to

> "outrage in the white communities of Arkansas and in the press across America. In the court of public opinion, the Cherokees were guilty for having their own independent system of justice. Subsequent cases of jurisdictional conflict, combined with a rising tide of white outlaws hiding in the Cherokee Nation, convinced many Americans that the days of tribal independence were numbered" (Blackburn, 2018, p. 135).

Note that both women mentioned in this story are identified as either current or past widows. Approximately 2.5 percent of the population of the United States, as a whole, died in the Civil War (PBS. *The Civil War by the Numbers*). The death toll in Indian Territory was much higher. "The Cherokee population apparently declined from 21,000 to 14,000 during the war period, a 33 percent loss. In addition to outright losses, countless widows and orphans created by the conflict underscored the disintegration of family life" (Confer, 2007, p. 145).

As far as we can find, all four Beck men noted as wounded or killed in the gunfight were eventually identified as Polly's nephews by other members of the family in testimonies, forms, and letters to the US Government. It's unclear if her nephews felt compelled by their fathers' traditional responsibility for their aunt's crying blood (Reid, 2006, p. 41) or just plain revenge. Some sources claim that, "The Cherokees believed that…spirits haunted the houses of relatives with whom the ultimate responsibility for vengeance lay…more of a family matter than foreign policy (Perdue, 1998, p. 52).

Bill Beck seems to have died before having any children or managing to be memorialized in Starr's work, and we couldn't find anyone of the next generation listing him among their uncles in the *Eastern Cherokee Applications of 1906-1909* available for online search by May of 2024. Charlotte Scott reported that her uncle, Samuel Beck, died without having children (Scott, Application Number 27, p. 5), and Emmet Starr noted that he married at least three times (p. 337). Both sources give Samuel's parents as Charlotte Downing and Ellis Beck. Their siblings lists match, which is why we believe these records identify the same Samuel.

While some records confuse the two, White Sut and Black Sut were the nicknames of cousins linked by their grandparents, Susannah Buffington and Jeffrey Beck. Jesse Surry Eaton "Black Sut" Beck's short life ended at the Goingsnake shootout. He was identified in Starr's work as Surry Eaton Beck, son of Joseph Beck and Cynthia Beck nee Downing, the 8th of 11 children (p. 337). His only child, John Beck, referred to him as Blacksoot Beck in Dawes Enrollment Jacket Card #6829 (p. 3). Black Sut was Julia Ann Beck's first husband. She reported, "My first husband's name was Jesse Beck. Now dead" (Eastern Cherokee Applications, Application No. 859, p. 5). His sister, Susannah Chandler nee Beck, called him "Jesse Beck" and gives his birth year as 1845 (p. 5).

White Sut escaped the scene of the trial and has become part of the "two guns" romantic Oklahoma history that Emmet Starr railed against in his history and genealogy work (Justice, 2006, p. 134). According to Starr, he was the son of Jeffrey Beck and Sallie Downing and married Susie Ellen Daniel (p. 343). He lived until about 1890 and is buried on Monkey Island with Susie under a carefully carved headstone. He managed his media image during his life, beginning with reports to an Arkansas newspaper while still recovering from the wounds taken at Goingsnake and describing himself as the "almost white" leader of the posse who "fired the second shot himself" (H.R. Exec. No. 287, 42nd Cong., 2nd Sess., 1872, p. 10). As we quote above, he even mentioned his aunt's murder in his dramatic arguments to his fellow citizens for Oklahoma statehood (Bell, J. and Beck, S.). His great-granddaughter, Pamela White, reports that he "settled down to a life of service to his family, community, and the Cherokee Nation" (p. 313).

To the twenty-first-century mind, drawing a gun over a stock dispute, or even coming to blows over it, may seem incredible. However, the recently ended war had a huge impact on livestock, which was both a source of wealth and provisions in pre-railroad Indian Territory.

> "Estimates place the number of cattle run out of Indian Territory into Kansas at 300,000 head, worth $4 million… the immediate consequence of the cattle raids for the Indians was the loss of a critical food supply and personal wealth that would never be recovered" (Confer, 2007, pp. 145–147).

The mill itself was one of the oldest mills in the relocated Cherokee Nation, having been built in 1845. "Millers not only provided valuable services to farmers…mills frequently served as community gathering places and post offices." (Baker et al., 2018, p. 76) It was both a grist and saw mill.

The district name, Goingsnake, isn't just an amusingly old-timey county moniker. Goingsnake district was one of the original eight geographic subdivisions established in 1840 in Indian

Territory by the Cherokee (Stremlau, 2011, p. 36). The region was named after a person, "Going Snake, a venerated elder statesman aligned with the Ross Party…born in approximately 1755…he led John Benge's contingent [on the Removal]" (Stremlau, 2011, pp. 36–37).

Allow us to bring you forward in time and introduce you to one of her great-grandson's favorite phrases.

"Tell them who you are."

Lisa relates:

That was our grandfather's frequent advice to his daughters and grandchildren. And it's how I started every conversation with many people as a child. Our maternal grandfather, L.C. Neel, was well known enough in our corner of Oklahoma that we soon learned the face people made as they spelled out the French "Neel" in their minds and replaced their assumed spelling: the more common English spelling "Neal." Our spelling was so uncommon in midwest America that it often led people to immediately identify us with our large family. In fact, I was in my 40s before I ever met another "Neel" living in the United States who wasn't my relative.

This has led to some tense moments, as perspectives on the trial are still diverse among Cherokee people.

During the second Chad Smith term as Cherokee Nation chief, I was on a site visit with my (non-Cherokee) boss to Tahlequah. I was the project manager on a federal grant for a non-profit organization.

Our host site director was driving us around. We started chit-chatting about our families, which is a very common Cherokee pastime. It's interesting to figure out how you might be related to someone. Since we don't formally use the clan system anymore, the talk tends to turn to immediate ancestry and lines of descent.

"So, you're a Neel. Is that your maiden name?"

"Yeah. I never took my husband's name. It was my mom's maiden name also. I'm L.C. Neel's granddaughter."

"Ooooooooh. So you're a *Neel* Neel. Whoo-eee."

"Yes. His mom was a Beck and through that line we're descended from Nancy Ward."

"Huh. Never knew some of the Neels are Becks. You're a Beck?"

The air in the car shifted a little. We were at a stop sign, and he turned to really look at me.

My boss said, "Wait…what's happening?"

"He's figuring out which side my family was on a treaty, two civil wars, and an…er…incident. I take it his family was on the other side of at least one."

At this, our host laughed and said, "Well…figures you're working with the Feds. I guess I already knew that."

"Well…your last name starts with a Mac so I assume you've got some other names, too."

"None as famous as yours."

I was puzzled. I had always thought of Nancy Ward as my famous ancestor and Polly as a simply tragic one. She survived the

Removal and died in a gunfight that wasn't her fault. How could that stain her name more than 100 years later?

I managed to turn the conversation to explain to my boss in general terms that the Northeast part of Indian Territory was a chaotic place that had been destroyed by the American Civil War after the Cherokee removal. I tried, in a few minutes, to summarize the "History of Cherokee Nation" course I had taken in 2003.

We closed the topic with our host saying, amicably, "Well, most of our White ancestors were sociopaths, which is why we only talk about the Cherokee ones."

So who *was* Polly Beck? Was she tragic or inspiring? Why has history largely skipped details about her in the telling of the story that opens with her death? The main details we can rely on come from her well-documented family tree.

As is common for many Americans descended from European settlers, it's hard to trace our grandfather's father's family tree very far beyond the 1860s without resorting to user-generated databases that, at best, piece together census records, military service records, and the occasional newspaper article.

This is in high contrast to our Cherokee ancestors, starting with L.C.'s mother, who was Polly's granddaughter, Willora. At the risk of beginning a long list of begats, we'd like to take a moment to outline Polly's documentable family tree. We don't have any documents written by her, but we have her children's and grandchildren's accounts of their family line, as well as a network of nieces, nephews, and other relatives. Some of the preserved documents are even in their own handwriting.

This contrast wasn't an accident, or because we care more about our Cherokee kin than our non-Cherokee relations. It's due to the intense scrutiny and deep surveillance of Cherokee citizens by the US empire in the nineteenth and early twentieth centuries.

Settlers have been counting Cherokee people since 1715, when the South Carolina colony estimated the size of the nation based on the reports of their traders (Reid, 2006, p. 6). The earliest English census of the whole Cherokee population was held in 1721 (Kelton, 2015, p. 211). Our story picks up again with two major sources that were produced in the nineteenth century: US Archives records related to Cherokee citizenship produced by the Dawes Commission and the work of Emmet Starr.

It turns out Henry Laurens Dawes (1816-1903) went to the same college I did, graduating 163 years before I did in 1839 (Fig. 1.2). He's buried in Pittsfield, MA. I visited his grave in mid-2024. His remains rest in a beautiful, parklike cemetery, overshadowed by a truly enormous gravestone with his wife, Electa Sanderson Dawes. When I say it's enormous, I'm not exaggerating. The stone with its plinth stands at least 6 or 7 feet high. The final inscription on the back of this stone reads, "Commissioner to the five tribes 1893-1903."

> "In 1896…Congress stripped the Cherokee Nation of its sovereign right to regulate tribal membership. Instead, it charged the Dawes Commission with creating a roster of the Cherokee Nation it…provide a complete list of those eligible to receive an allotment…organize the population into categories…[and] facilitate the transmission of newly privatized property through sale and inheritance in the future" (Stremlau, 2011, p. 110).

Fig. 1.2 Henry Laurens Dawes headstone with Lisa for scale. Photo by Elspeth Neel-Lewis.

What the Dawes commission accomplished was to create

"a document that has immeasurably shaped modern-day Americans' understanding of who Cherokees are…

it has fostered enormous misunderstanding about Cherokee culture…it reflects a non Indian definition of tribal membership from a moment in American history when Anglo-Americans understood indigenous people to be less than fully human" (Stremlau, 2011, p. 148).

Julia Ann Bee nee Hilderbrand enrolled with the Dawes Commission when she was 48 in 1900 (National Archives Catalog. Dawes Enrollment Jacket for Cherokee, Cherokee by Blood, Card #6834). Enrollment card number 6834 shows the administrative hand of the Dawes commission's attempt to divide Cherokee families into nuclear units, placing her as the head of her family, including herself and the four children living in her home at the time. Her oldest son enrolled himself separately on card 6829. Her testimony describing her children and their three fathers suggests she practiced the marital "fluidity rather than permanence" common among her peers and kinspeople (Stremlau, 2011, p. 53).

Her enrollment date before 1902 suggests she may have reported to the commission willingly (Stremlau, 2011, p. 107). The fact that they allotted her land directly suggests they saw her as the head of her household and assigned her a relatively low blood quantum due to their own assumptions "correlating blood quantum and competence" (Stremlau, 2011, p. 194).

Julia A. Bee nee Hilderbrand's later application for $133.19 under the "Eastern Cherokee Judgment, 1906–1911" fortunately for us, required her to provide the English and Cherokee names of her grandparents and list all of their children as well as she could. As a legal document with money attached, it was reviewed and matched with other US records before being accepted by the US Court of Claims. Founded in 1855, in 1902 an act of Congress,

> "gave the Court of Claims jurisdiction over any claim arising under treaty stipulations that the Cherokee Tribe, or any band thereof, might have against the United States and over any claims that the United States might have against any Cherokee Tribe or band" (National Archives Trust Fund Board, 1981, p. 1).

Julia Ann's document, Application Number 859, packs a huge amount of information into 26 pages. The bureaucratic form bursts with lists of names and "ditto" marks (Eastern Cherokee Applications, Application No. 859, pp. 1–26).

An index card tucked on top of the record hints at a web of living relatives also seeking to draw funds by listing 54 other records (seven of these have been struck out). Written in the era before the Court used ballpoint pens, the paper, now available as a digitized scan, includes some light writing in pencil but mostly bears the deep marks of metal nibs.

Julia Ann's application serves as an index of several other rolls because "In certifying the eligibility of the Cherokees, Miller used earlier census lists and rolls that had been made of the Cherokees by Hester, Chapman, Drennen, and others between 1835 and 1884" (National Archives Trust Fund Board, 1981, p. 3). It is also connected to the aforementioned 54 other records.

This form even obliquely mentions the events of 1872. Julia Ann gives her mother's death date of February 13, 1872, and notes that, "My first husband's name was Jesse Beck. Now dead."

Julia A. Bee, nee Julia A. Hilderbrand,

Cherokee Name: Quah-la-yuke

Born: July 20, 1852

Stephen Hilderbrand, Sr., Julia's father

Cherokee Name: Cun-aga-yun

Born in Tennessee

Died: January 10, 1867

Polly Hilderbrand [nee Beck], also noted as "Mary or Polly", Julia's mother

No Cherokee name given.

Born in Georgia

Susannah Beck, later Susannah Eaton, nee Buffington, Polly's mother

No Cherokee name given.

Born in Georgia

Jeffrey Beck, Sr., Polly's father

No Cherokee name given.

Born in Georgia

Julia Ann provided 18 uncles and aunts, which gives us a glimpse into a large family, many of whom were born in the early nineteenth century. She reported that all of them had died by the time she filled out the form.

The form itself might even be filled out in Julia Ann's handwriting and is filed along with a two-page letter from her to the

Commissioner of Indian Affairs dated January 19, 1907. The application was approved, but the receipts included in the surviving record report that payments were made out to three members of her family: Willora C. J. Neel nee Bee, John Beck, and Charles Wafford.

The US Treasury also got a share.

Julia died March 21, 1907, without a will disposing of her estate, which consisted entirely of her Cherokee allotment (Ancestry.com Operations, Inc. 2015). Her probate record, settled on April 24, 1914, shows the transition to Oklahoma State jurisdiction was complete. The married name of her fourth child, Willora, is misspelled as Neil.

Julia Ann's list of Polly's half-siblings: Dick, Harlin, Suzie, and Charlotte provide a solid link to Polly's stepfather: Surry (sometimes spelled Surrey) Eaton.

Surry Eaton was among the men indicted in September of 1831 by the grand jury of Gwinnett County, Georgia, "for the offense of residing within the limits of the Cherokee nation without a license" (Ramage, 1902, p. 205). Students of Supreme Court history will remember the name of one of his co-defendants: Samuel Austin Worcester. Surry must have been one of the men, "tried and convicted in a state superior court and sentenced to four years of hard labor at the state penitentiary. All but two of them…pledged not to violate the law again and accepted a pardon from the governor" (Saunt, 2020, p. 162).

Emmet Starr's work lists Surry as Susannah's second husband (Starr, 1921, p. 305). We could not find any evidence he was related to the American secretary of war, John Eaton.

We don't usually concern ourselves with stepfathers in family trees despite our own close relationship with our stepfather (sorry, Dad!), but in this case Polly was probably living in his household in 1835 and therefore was one of the people mentioned in the census: "Six Cherokees, 5 quarterbloode, 5 [enslaved people], 1 white intermarriage, 1 farmer, 2 readers of English, 1 weaver, 2 spinsters" (Foreman, 1971, p. 160).

Luckily for us, Emmet's reports overlap with Julia's family list by one generation and stretch well into the early eighteenth century, even though he was about the same age as her oldest child. Dr. Starr's books are often the first resource people use to explore Cherokee family trees. The web of the remaining family members in Polly's maternal line is documented in Starr's compact way on Page 305 of his *History of the Cherokee Indians and Their Legends and Folk Lore* published in 1921.

In summary, it boils down to:

Ezekial Buffington, Susannah's father

Mary Buffington nee Emory, Susannah's mother

Mary Emory nee Grant, Mary's Buffington's mother

William Emory, Mary Buffington's father

Ludovic Grant, Mary Emory's father

Some of his letters to the colonial governor of South Carolina have been preserved (JSTOR, 2024).

Starr does not record Mary Emory's mother's name, but all sources mentioning her were confident that she was Cherokee.

This family tree formed our main lens for considering how Polly might have presented herself in the world as she lived her life through a difficult, uncertain time period in Cherokee history.

These news reports, administrative documents, court records, and testimonies gave us a start on learning more about Polly as a person. We continued to explore her life as a woman, Cherokee citizen, and skilled worker while evaluating our own assumptions about Cherokee people from this time.

It may be impossible to peer into the past as clearly as we would like. We have no way of really knowing many details of events. However, in telling as much of Polly's story as clearly as we are able and attempting to, so to speak, step into her shoes, we hope to shed some light into a dark corner that previously appeared to be a quagmire of blood and violence.

2
Cherokee culture in the nineteenth century: Negotiation, self-presentation, and calico dresses

Looking back, I feel very fortunate that I was introduced to the possibility that a Cherokee person could feel trapped or caught between two worlds when I was nearly an adult. Growing up, I was generally aware that some families lived "more traditionally" than mine did. I just didn't think of it as a problem I might have to solve or explain until I was in Jace Weaver's 1998 Native American Literature course. We covered a huge body of literature that often concerned itself with the problem of walking in two worlds. I remember Jace quite fondly, although now I cringe a little at the way I acted in his classes. In my horrified memory, I blurted interjections and sputtered through entire class sessions, coming to grips with the possibility that native identity could be a bifurcation rather than a continuum. I remember once literally whipping my Cherokee Identification card (at the time, still just a flimsy piece of cardboard) out of my wallet to show a fellow student doubting my citizenship. Jace was the only Cherokee professor on campus and was very patient with my involved "audience participation" in his lectures.

As Lara and I worked on understanding Polly Beck's context, I was happy to find his familiar name referenced and thanked by many sources. I enjoyed revisiting his work more than 20 years after I first read it. A fresh publication in 1998, "That the People Might Live" was a wonderful introduction to the rich and complex body of literature that Native people have published. It gave me my first viewpoint into a Cherokee history larger than my immediate experience and gave me some of the concepts I needed to explain my complex nationality to outsiders.

Many Euro-American historians frame Cherokee cultural identity as a defined space. As if a person moves from one culture to the next by walking through a door. We'd like to offer a Cherokee-centered perspective, in which culture is a spiraling umbrella, expanding to include new things. The living Cherokee culture expands and adapts. It always has. As Jace writes, "It is important to insist that Native cultures be seen as living, dynamic cultures" (Weaver, 1997, p. 8). Depictions of it as breaking, fading, or being abandoned due to outmarriage or taking up new technologies are colonialist fantasies. Reading sources through that perspective revealed that Polly may have felt just as we do, if she thought of the potential conflict at all.

I must also address a word that is often anathema in non-white American spaces. "Assimilation" is often conflated with capitulation to white supremacy by giving up a non-white identity. However, Cherokee journalist Rebecca Nagle points out that adoption of majority cultural norms was a form of self-preservation.

> "From the time of George Washington, US presidents promised Cherokees that if they could live more like white people – raise livestock, farm, wear cotton clothes, and adopt Christianity – they could remain on their lands. For Cherokees, the pressure to assimilate was also practical. There was not enough wild game to support subsistence hunting, so more Cherokees kept livestock. After tides of death from disease, intermarrying with white people helped Cherokees rebuild their population…over and over again, Cherokees adapted" (2024, p. 61).

Nineteenth century Cherokee identities: Adaptation, expansion, and boundaries

While "On the surface Cherokees appeared to rapidly and thoroughly adopt Euro-American culture during the early 19th century…hunting gave way to livestock herding as the most important economic activity for Cherokee men…Cherokee women meanwhile eagerly took to cloth production" (Kelton, 2015, p. 177), Cherokee tradition is flexible enough to include new technologies and lifeways without losing itself. As Theda Perdue wrote, "In the nineteenth century, Cherokees incorporated aspects of Anglo-American culture into their lives without fundamentally altering values or totally restructuring gender" (Perdue, 1998, p. 9).

Missionary observers of the eighteenth and nineteenth centuries certainly thought the link between religion, lifestyle, and proximity to whiteness was very strong. One "Baptist missionary remarked that, 'though their skin is red, or dark, I assure you, their mental powers are white'" (Perdue, 1998, p. 162).

By the late 1820s, the missionaries of the Brainerd mission, working under the American Board of Commissioners of Foreign Missions, operated eight schools in the Cherokee Nation, educating as many as 200 children at a time. "A typical school day began at 5:30 a.m. and ended at 9:00 p.m…students were required to perform gender-specific labor tasks…chores such as dressmaking and cooking for the girls" (Carney, 2005, p. 47).

The United States' attempts to force cultural change on all tribes during the assimilation era reflected reformers' views "conflating domestic work and civilization…that made household labor into not just a set of tasks but a ladder of progress" (Simonsen, 2006, p. 217). In the late nineteenth century, reformers even sent Native women boxes of fabric and materials and began formally "teaching them skills like sewing and decorative needlework…[the Native] women's handiwork symbolized the success of assimilationist policies" (Stremlau, 2011, p. 87). As usual, I blame the people of the late nineteenth century for distorting our twenty-first-century viewpoint.

We do not believe that our ancestors shared this viewpoint.

> "In no way, though, did the Valley Towns represent one side of a bifurcated Cherokee Nation, one in which poor, monolingual, subsistence farmers stood in opposition to wealthy, bicultural, commercially oriented slaveholders.

> These two archetypes instead occupied two ends of a spectrum of diverse Cherokee communities" (Kelton, 2015, p. 178).

For a more detailed analysis of the Cherokee cultural dynamic of balance between frank resistance and harmony, we recommend the work of Daniel Heath Justice.

As Wilma Mankiller observed, "Indigenous people have long understood how to move in and out of parallel universes and maintain their cultural values" (Mankiller, 2004, p. 7).

Writing in the early nineteenth century, Colonel Return J. Meigs recounted a conversation with a Cherokee named Eskaqua, or Bloody Fellow, that sums it up well.

> "[Bloody Fellow said that] even should the habits and customs of the Cherokees give place to the habits & customs of whites, or even should they themselves become white by intermarriage, not a drop of Indian blood would be lost; it would be spread more widely, but not lost." (McLoughlin, 1984, p. 24)

Rose Stremlau observed in her book examining the impact of twentieth-century allotment on a group of Cherokee families that, "Cherokee families had proven remarkably able to incorporate elements of non-Indian culture into their way of life and yet remain committed to core values that shaped the way they interacted with one another" (Stremlau, 2011, p. 6). Further, "For many assimilationists, the Cherokees were proof that Indians could learn to live like Anglo-Americans…by the late 19th Century, however, it was clear that Cherokees did not want to assimilate fully" (Stremlau, 2011, p. 73).

Further, "Cherokee statesmen refuted the suggestion that their society had evolved to its greatest capacity…they insisted that the development of Cherokee civilization was a process of continual adaptation…their time-tested way of life…did not replace traditional Cherokee culture but perfected it" (Stremlau, 2011, p. 100). As Parins recently observed, "George Washington's "civilization policy" as it became known, drew many of the same conclusions that the Cherokee leadership adopted, although for different reasons" (Parins, 2003, p. 14). Cherokees, as a whole, adapted many trappings of "civilization" not to wipe away the barbarism White Americans projected on us, but because we wanted to do so.

It's important to avoid the mistake of conflating cultural change with assimilation. Even among very liberal white Americans, the possibility that Native Americans could live among them was a fringe idea until the very late nineteenth century. Nor was it the goal of Cherokee reformers and thought leaders. The unusually well-educated original editor of the Cherokee Phoenix newspaper, Elias Boudinot (nee Buck Watie), published *An Address to the Whites Delivered in the First Presbyterian Church, on the 26th of May 1826* in which he stated, "As [Cherokees] rise in information and refinement, changes in [our government] must follow, until they arrive at that state of advancement, when I trust they will be admitted into all the privileges of the American family" (Perdue, 1996, pp. 74–75). Theda Perdue clarified in her gloss of his writing, "Boudinot did not mean assimilation. He believed that when the Cherokee government had reached a certain level of sophistication, the Cherokee people as a distinct political entity would enjoy the rights and privileges of other Americans" (Perdue, 1996,

p. 81). Please note, this was six years before Boudinot's philosophical break from John Ross, when he was still the leader of the government-funded and -controlled newspaper.

We have inherited these attitudes that persist among living Cherokee people. As Jace Weaver reports, "The Cherokees of *Faces in the Moon* maintain their identity and their culture no matter how assimilated they appear to their Amer-European neighbors" (Weaver, 1997, p. 158). Insisting otherwise is a "convenient erasure and removal of Native presence that traps Indians as unchanging museum artifacts instead of human communities with dynamic traditions and historically influenced cultural contexts" (Justice, 2006, p. 122).

The 1984 analysis conducted by McLoughlin of the 1830s censuses supports this by documenting that wealth, skills, and literacy were widespread in Cherokee families regardless of their history of marriages to White Americans (1984, p. 246). As McLoughlin notes,

> "it appears from the census that the Cherokee were moving toward the prevailing white frontier practice of the nuclear family living on its own subsistence farm. This was certainly what the federal agents and missionaries encouraged…even the full-blood families were acculturating…acculturation enforced by the decline of their old economy of hunting, farming, fishing, and gathering" (1984, pp. 236–237).

We'll probably repeat this a few times, but it bears repeating. When you're reading nineteenth-century sources about Cherokee people, the issue of blood quantum always comes up. It lurks in the background and misleads modern readers into accepting the implicit assumption that there was a clear distinction between full-blood and mixed-blood Cherokees' culture, language, and abilities. You don't have to be a believer in the Solutrean hypothesis (Saini, 2019, p. 131) or need the picture book, "Not My Idea: A Book about Whiteness" (Higginbotham, 2018), to be infected by the racialized ideas that are so thoroughly baked into the sources.

Intermarriage with White Americans was not even associated with English speaking. They didn't co-occur or require one for the other. Kelton explains the conflation:

> "The social makeup and political world of the Cherokee Nation in the 1870s were certainly complex. Unfortunately…the "full-blood" and "mixed-blood" dichotomy emphasized by the enemies of Indian sovereignty…were constructs that Cherokee rarely used themselves but that appeared frequently in US government records. For example, federal agents broke down Cherokee population statistics by blood, recording that in 1879 there were 6,000 "mixed-bloods" and 8,000 "full-bloods" …Since government officials had no definite way of telling who had European ancestry and who did not, they often used cultural characteristics as a means to categorize people. Cherokee who adopted Euro-American customs, especially language, were assumed to have European ancestors. Of course, such assumptions are based on the false idea that race determines culture, and for that reason I will not employ the terms "full-blood" and "mixed-blood" to put Cherokee into two different cultural groups" (2003, p. 16).

Daniel Heath Justice explains this persistent Cherokee perspective, "The terms fullblood, mixedblood, traditional, and progressive are often used as absolute terms...such absolutes are rarely accurate...Degree of blood quantum should not be read as a measure of commitment to Cherokee nationhood or identification as Cherokee" (Justice, 2006, p. xv). "Our long history of intermarriage, adaptation, and innovative accommodation has brought a wide range of physical features, cultural practices, languages, and ideas into our varied understandings of what it is to be Cherokee, and we thrive as a result" (Justice, 2006, p. 6).

In the late nineteenth century, "Cherokees spoke their own language of blood...they used the term "full blood" to refer to those who spoke Cherokee as their primary language...the term referred not to heritage but to one's lifestyle" (Stremlau, 2011, pp. 142–143). Like many other things in our culture, there's a bit of a spiral in it.

> "The Cherokee conception of who was considered a full-blood and who a mixed blood differed from the commonly held blood-quantum idea...the criteria were linguistic and cultural rather than racial or biological. A full-blood was any person whose primary and preferred language was Cherokee, even though the subject might have had a white ancestor" (Parins, 2003, p. 20).

Conversely, as Mary Evelyn Rogers noted, "White genes did not carry white culture, and outward adaptation to white civilization did not carry with it the abandonment of the Cherokee outlook" (Stremlau, 2011, p. 14).

Justice further points out the irony in nineteenth century blood quantum calculations made by the United States when evaluating Cherokee people on a spectrum of presumed competence.

> "Those with higher amounts of Indian "blood" were accorded more legitimacy as Indians, but this often resulted in alternate U.S. discrimination via "competency" designations…Indians with lower blood quanta were often permitted full title to their allotments, while those with higher quanta were frequently marked as incompetent" (Justice, 2006, p. 99).

The White American assessment of Cherokee blood quantum wasn't even based on observed phenotype or self-report through questioning, but on the judgment of individual census takers and overworked commission clerks. This can be demonstrated by comparing designations of individuals and families over time, where individuals could be identified by clerks as increasingly white as they gained education and business acumen (Stremlau, 2011, pp. 204–205).

We have not found Cherokee-sourced evidence that Cherokees generally shared such beliefs in the eighteenth and nineteenth centuries. The missionary John Gambold wrote in 1810: "All the children of white men raised with Indian mothers belong without question to the family and lineage of the mother" (Miles, 2010, p. 42).

Cherokee contact with Europeans began as early as 1540 during the Hernando DeSoto expedition, and regular contact with English speakers began in the late seventeenth century (King, 2007, p. xiv). As early as the mid-eighteenth century, white traders routinely lived in Cherokee towns and "married or cohabited with women from prominent families…the offspring of some of these families grew up in homes that were bilingual and bicultural" (King, 2007, pp. xv–xvii). European, then Euro-American men marrying Cherokee women and having families in the Cherokee Nation did not challenge Cherokee conceptions of family structure or clan government, although it did create jurisdictional issues that the Nation grappled with in various ways through the nineteenth century and beyond. Cherokee citizenship was not originally seen as racially based by Cherokees, but as something inherited from the mother (Perdue, 1998, p. 82).

Meanwhile, White American ideas of race and nationhood were becoming more rigid and protective of whiteness.

> "By the early nineteenth century, the increasing reliance [among white people] on biological notions of race had rendered the idea of interracial sexual contact unnatural and repugnant…while the white man/native woman relationship was consonant with the impetus of colonization, the converse posed an almost unrecoverable threat…the status of white women functioned to stabilize whiteness as a racial identity" (Gaul, 2005, p. 11).

The antimiscegenation sentiment was so strong in Connecticut in 1825 that when Harriet Gold became engaged to the Cherokee Elias Boudinot nee Buck Watie, her beloved brother Stephen burned her in effigy and participated in a riot in the Cornwall village green (Gaul, 2005, p. 1). Elias' clear admiration of "civilization," his fine clothes, his sincere conversion to Christianity, and his education were not enough to make him an accepted peer of the Puritan "Bachelors of 'Cornwall Valley'" (Gabriel, 1941, p. 63).

Harriet was not the first white American woman to marry a Cherokee man, but a relatively large volume of her letters and notes were preserved by her family, so much so that nearly half of the biography of Elias written by Ralph Henry Gabriel in 1941 is really about his in-laws. It's convenient for us that she gave her family a glimpse into Cherokee interest in textile work through her letters, noting that, "Her skills in sewing were in much demand among the Cherokees, who were increasingly dressing in Western attire but did not necessarily have the domestic skills to match their desires" (Gaul, 2005, p. 53). Her family's shopping list early in her marriage included finished clothes for her husband, fabric specifically for "little girls," shoes for herself, and sewing supplies, including "1 pair of mantuamaker's shears" (Gaul, 2005, pp. 73–74). While her skills were in demand, she had company for sewing already, as she reported to her sister that her Cherokee mother-in-law, "cuts and makes all the clothes for her family except the coats for the men" (Gaul, 2005, p. 154).

Meanwhile, the Cherokee Nation responded to these marriages by enlarging its conception of citizenship to include families with naturalized Cherokee mothers of European-American descent, creating a revised, racially informed but not racially bound national identity. In 1825, the council "extended Cherokee citizenship to 'the children of Cherokee men and white women, living in the Cherokee Nation as man and wife'" (Perdue, 1998, p. 147). This did not fully overthrow clan-based systems, as the Cherokee Council upheld the rights of several notable adopted citizens in the late 1830s (Perdue, 1998, pp. 150–151).

We have to be clear that this wasn't a race-blind, utopian society. Tiya Miles has documented how this widening of citizenship and formal regulation of intermarried whites promulgated the race-oriented hierarchy practiced in the neighboring communities of the United States.

> "Cherokee law differentiated between Cherokees, blacks, and whites, but it did so in a way that elevated the position of whites in the Nation over that of blacks. In the context of the strategic Cherokee nationalism of the 1820's, the Nation's leaders used race as a determining factor for deciding who did and did not belong in the Cherokee Nation, and they seared these racialized definitions into law" (Miles, 2015b, p. 111).

Specifically,

> "children of Cherokee men and free women, except women of African descent, would be granted citizenship. Children of Cherokee women and 'all free men' remained citizens; however, the progeny of marital unions between Cherokee women and free men of African descent would be granted incomplete and restricted Cherokee citizenship" (Naylor, 2008, p. 13).

Possibly ironically,

> "the same body of laws that had narrowed the definition of Cherokee citizenship when it came to black people had broadened that definition when it came to patrilineality…the Cherokee Constitution had included the children of Cherokee men and nonblack, free women as members of the Nation" (Miles, 2015b, p. 128).

This legal change may be less of a departure than it first appears. Under the clan system in the eighteenth century,

> "any person, regardless of ancestry or nationality, who was born or adopted into one of the seven clans was a Cherokee; any person who did not belong to a Cherokee clan was not a member of the tribe and was liable to be killed almost at a whim" (Purdue, 1998, p. 49).

Cherokees never limited citizenship to people with only Cherokee parents. Tiya Miles notes, "In the Cherokee context...enslaved women and men would have been particularly vulnerable to abuse- not because the law sanctioned their abuse as it did in white society, but because the protection of Cherokee kinship structure did not extend to them" (Miles, 2015b, p. 51).

At the same time that Cherokee citizenship was expanding to include more people, active participation of those citizens in chattel slavery was increasing. Enslavement was also becoming formalized, with the Cherokee Council passing laws in the 1820s to restrict the movements and activities of people held in bondage by Cherokee citizens, "lending state support" to the authority of enslavers (Miles, 2010, p. 165). This state support extended to specific laws such as an 1825 statute outlawing rape, "a law that did not explicitly exclude [enslaved] women, as did rape laws in the United States" (Miles, 2015b, p. 54). This appears to be intentional, as "other Cherokee laws passed in the 1820's did differentiate between "Negro slaves," Cherokees, and whites" (Miles, 2015b, p. 54).

The package of "civilization" that some Euro-Americans promoted to the Cherokee people included the practice of chattel-style slavery (Miles, 2010, p. 111), with some observers specifically linking Cherokee "advances" to it. In 1859, the federal agent to the

Cherokee Nation noted, "I am clearly of the opinion that the rapid advancement of the Cherokees is owing in part to the fact of their being slaveholders, which has operated as an incentive to all industrial pursuits" (Powell, 1887, p. 322). He was correct about the link between slaveholding and growing cash crops, but he had the correlation backward. As Perdue notes, "Only when the identification of women with agriculture had ended was the introduction and utilization of slave labor for cultivation by even a minority of Cherokees possible" (1979, p. 53).

Rebecca Nagle makes the connection between the losses of Indigenous land and enslavement clear.

> "Most often the histories of Indigenous dispossession and enslavement in the United States are taught separately, but these two systems of oppression needed each other. What we think of as the antebellum or Deep South was built on the land Southern lawmakers fought for and won in the Indian Removal Act. And in 1830, the South had an additional 21 votes in the House, because enslaved people – who of course could not vote – were counted toward Southern states' representation. Without those 21 votes, the bill would have never passed" (2024, p. 74).

Slaveholding wasn't limited to one especially decadent or privileged group of Cherokee people. Even if we accept the assignment from census workers of "family type" [blood quantum assessments made by American census takers]: 7.4 percent of all households in the Cherokee Nation enslaved at least one person (McLoughlin, 1984, p. 228). Slaveholding wasn't limited to large plantations and therefore only to cotton production: 2.5 percent of all Cherokee households surveyed held 1 or 2 people in bondage (McLoughlin, 1984, p. 245).

Put a pin in our assertion that enslavement of other people was unremarkable among Cherokee people by the early nineteenth century. We'll explore the continued effects of this on the Cherokee Nation and our own work to accept and depict Polly's reality related to enslavement in Chapter 3.

We hope we have convinced you that cultural adaptation was independent from intermarriage with White Americans and that both of these realities were incorporated into the lives of nineteenth century Cherokee people as part of their living culture. We don't mean to suggest that the Cherokee Nation was completely unified any more than any other society can be. As Carey Vicenti put it,

> "the most powerful and significant social consequence of [removal] treaties was that they had a tendency to drive a wedge into tribal society and create two different political factions…you get this lingering dichotomy in tribal politics, in which you have people who engage in concessions with the federal government and people who resist" (Harjo, 2014, p.85).

Divisions creating dead Cherokees, live Cherokees, and legal Cherokees

"Indians come in all sorts of social and historical configurations. North American popular culture is littered with savage, noble, and dying Indians, while in real life we have Dead Indians, Live Indians, and Legal Indians" (King, 2013, p. 53).

Any summary of the settler colonialism of the American empire mentions the Cherokee Removal as part of one of the main sins of the early Republic, often as a regrettable but inevitable consequence of Manifest Destiny. There are so many books and articles about the Cherokee Removal that, as an event, it almost suffers from overexposure. "White Americans liked to think that the mass deportation of the 1830's and the westward-moving line that it created were inevitable" (Saunt, 2020, p. 318).

The live Cherokee relationship with the Removal is complicated. Depending on the context, it can evoke inspiration, rage, or even guilt. It's the topic of frequently staged works of performance art produced by Cherokee organizations for the general public, most famously the companion plays, "Unto these Hills" and "Trail of Tears," written by Dr. Kermit Hunter (O'Dell, n.d.). One of the actors in some of the 1970s Trail of Tears seasons later wrote, "It was a white man's version of Indian history, told simplistically, if sympathetically, with spectacular special effects- dance! music! costumes! flash pots in the Civil War scenes!" (This Land Press, 2017, p. 138).

The Cherokee Nation even hosts a well-publicized bicycle ride commemorating the Removal.

> "The Remember the Removal Bike Ride was started by the Cherokee Nation in 1984 for Cherokee youth to retrace the Trail of Tears and get a glimpse of the hardships their ancestors faced when they made the same trek on foot years before…The ride became an annual

event starting in 2009 and the Eastern Band of Cherokee Indians joined the ride in 2011" (Cherokee.org).

Most of my life, I have taken comfort from the strength I presumed my ancestors displayed during the removal and the rebuilding of our nation in Indian Territory. Any discussion of Cherokee families through the nineteenth century would be incomplete without it as key context.

While commemorations, discussions, and apologies focus on the Removal as if it occurred at one point in time, it was actually a long process (Saunt, 2020) that ultimately shaped the development of a kind of cultural Venn diagram. To borrow from Thomas King's concept of "Dead Indians, Live Indians, and Legal Indians," we started to view our Cherokee ancestors through these three cultural facets: Dead Cherokees were romanticized memories, Live Cherokees are living people with a distinct culture and nationhood, and Legal Cherokees are defined by the intersection between jurisdiction and nationhood. Legal Cherokees are a subset of Live Cherokees with legal citizenship recognized by the United States federal government, including descendants of formerly enslaved and free individuals.

Ruth Margaret Muskrat Bronson and the American cultural memory of nineteenth-century Cherokees

Ruth Margaret Muskrat Bronson is a good figure to help us transition from the crushing scope of the Removal to the individual level. She was a poet, author, advocate, and educator (Fig. 2.1).

In 2023, the Cherokee Phoenix reported that, "the Cherokee Nation celebrated the centennial of Bronson's visit to the White House in Washington D.C., when as a 27-year-old, she represented Native American leaders from the Committee of 100, presented a copy of Gustavus Elmer Emmanuel Lindquist's book "The Red Man in the United States" to President Calvin Coolidge and gave a speech on Indian policy, all while wearing regalia that reflected pan-Indian cultural identity. To celebrate the 100-year anniversary, Bronson's family donated her regalia and original speech to the Cherokee National Research Center and CN officials declared Dec. 13 as Ruth Muskrat Bronson Day in the Cherokee Nation'" (Cherokee Phoenix, 2023b).

In 1944 she published a book, "Indians are People, Too." The title alone suggests a level of ongoing cultural dissociation: her American audience needed a reminder of her own humanity in 1944.

It's unclear why Ruth Margaret chose to dress in a "pan-Indian" buckskin for such public appearances in the 1920s (Fig. 2.1). It could be that she was deliberately invoking the Dead Indian trope as described by Thomas King in his book, *The Inconvenient Indian*. Whether or not they were aware of it, Sacheen Littlefeather, Senator Benjamin Nighthorse Campbell, W. Richard West, Jr., and Phil Fontaine have all dressed as the Dead Indian of the American imagination just like Ruth Margaret did,

> "war bonnets, beaded shirts, fringed deerskin dresses, loincloths, headbands, feathered lances, tomahawks, moccasins, face paint, and bone chokers. These bits of

Fig 2.1 Ruth Muskrat Bronson, promotional photo. Archives and Special Collections at Mount Holyoke College. Used with kind permission.

cultural debris- authentic and constructed- are what literary theorists like to call "signifiers," signs that create a "simulacrum" …something that represents something that never existed" (King, 2013, p. 54).

This trope is best summed up through the work of Iron Eyes Cody with the National Ad Council as the Crying Indian, "By the early 1970's, then, Iron Eyes Cody[3] was not only simply a Native American character actor, but one of the most important figures in fashioning Americans' ideas about the 'authentic Indian'" (This Land Press, 2017, p. 147).

"Dead Indians are dignified, noble, silent, suitably garbed. And dead. Live Indians are invisible, unruly, disappointing. And breathing. One is a romantic reminder of a heroic but fictional past. The other is simply an unpleasant, contemporary surprise" (King, 2013, p. 66).

Dead Indians are so enmeshed in modern American culture that they show up as tropes in horror movies and make guest appearances in the background in ghost tours. In such tours, "native people were present only as part of the landscape, existing before history rather than within it and creating the surface upon which the dramas of other groups would later play out" (Miles, 2015, p. 125).

Ruth Margaret's life intersects with this history partly because her writing and advocacy centered the poetic label of "Trail of Tears" and permanently associated it with the Removal. The Smithsonian National Museum of the American Indian's display about the Removal reported, "1914: A new generation of Native activists emerges...Ruth Muskrat Bronson writes a poem called "Trail of Tears." For public appearances she plays to popular misconceptions and deliberately wears Plains Indian, rather than Cherokee, attire" (Smithsonian National Museum of the American Indian Exhibit: Nation to Nation: Treaties Between the United States and American Indian Nations).

Polly's removal story: The suits of legal Cherokees

Polly's removal story may not have included significant loss of individuals or material wealth. She most likely emigrated with the Surry Eaton family. We have been unable to find their specific names on any muster lists, so we can't prove it.

We know a little more about the removal story of her future husband, Stephen Hildebrand. Stephen would have been in his early 20s in 1838. According to family oral history, Stephen joined his uncle, Peter Hildebrand, on what is now known as the "Hildebrand route" of the removal.

We can't know exactly how she traveled from the original Cherokee Nation (in what became Georgia) to Indian Territory (in what became Oklahoma). We know she did, and that in doing so, she was a "live Indian" who transformed into a "legal Indian" through that journey and the web of relationships she formed in her life.

Stitching it all together: Cherokee women's adoption of European-American clothing and textile skills

When we started looking for details on what Cherokee women wore in this period, we thought we already knew the answer.

The twentieth-century Tear Dress is as authentic and culturally significant to living Cherokee people as any other nation's historically informed folk dress. Often made of printed cotton today, the full shirtwaist style dominates the modern Cherokee imagination of our own past, appearing in many depictions of women in the time period, such as Dorothy Sullivan's "But This Is My Home," painted in 1998 (Fitzgerald, 2002, p. 46). Tonia Hogner-Weavel, a Cherokee National Treasure and textiles expert, explained in her presentation on Cherokee Traditional Dress (Hogner-Weavel, 2019) that a committee of dressmakers developed the Tear Dress in the late 1960s based on an extant antique purported to have been brought to Indian Territory by a survivor of the Removal.

Tonia's comments made us seek out specific descriptions of Cherokee people drawn from life in the nineteenth century. We ended up finding overwhelming textual evidence that Cherokee women had access to choices in European-style clothing by the early nineteenth century and may have been wearing entirely European-style clothes by the mid-nineteenth century, as we found several references to our people already seeking European-style clothes in the eighteenth century.

Early European depictions of Native people gave the impression that we started out almost naked. "An icon of a man dressed only in leaves was impressed in wax on the earliest official documents of the Massachusetts Bay Colony...yet writers who emphasized Indian nakedness sometimes described Indian clothing in some detail" (Ulrich, 2001, p. 54).

As early as 1745, the Cherokee Skiagunsta wrote to the governor of South Carolina: "My people cannot live independent [sic] of the English...The clothes we wear we cannot make ourselves..." (Miles, 2010, p. 43).

Speaking in 1754, a Cherokee headman "described his people's relationship with Governor Glen of South Carolina...'he always desired them to hunt briskly to kill plenty of Deer, that with the Skins they might buy Cloaths for their Wives...'" (Perdue, 1998, p. 76).

> "Based on descriptions ca. 1760, Cherokee women's clothing included a shirt made of linen or calico, a wrap-around skirt, and side-seam leggings made of wool stroud trade cloth and decorated with silk ribbons and beads. Cherokee women also wore linen waistcoats decorated with beads and shells and calico linen or cotton petticoats" (King, 2007, p. 26).

In the spring of 1819, the naturalist Thomas Nuttall "gives an interesting account of the western Cherokee [Old Settlers] ...their dress was a mixture of indigenous and European taste" (Mooney, 2009, p. 133). This note was especially intriguing to us, since the Old Settlers "emigrated to the new territory, hoping to preserve their traditional way of life and remove themselves from white influence" (Parins, 2003, p. 47). These relatively conservative, even nationalist, Cherokees, incorporated Euro-American styles in their dress even as they sought to escape the American empire.

"By the late eighteenth century, Cherokee women had universally adopted the modest skirts, blouses, and shawls commonly worn by Anglo-American women" (Perdue, 1998, p. 166). While Dr. Perdue's writing shows a silhouette-oriented understanding of nineteenth century White American dress, we were tantalized by her description and kept looking for more sources.

Writing in 1828, Elias Boudinot nee Buck Watie editorialized, "There was a time within our remembrance…when it was thought a disgrace, for a Cherokee to appear in the costume of a white man" (Perdue, 1996, p. 94). Writing in 1830, he boasted, "Cut off the last vestige of game in these woods [of Georgia], and you cannot starve the Cherokees – they have plenty of corn, and domestic animals, and they raise their own cotton and manufacture their own clothing" (Perdue, 1996, p. 115).

Women do not always dress in the same style as their male relatives, but we had to start with visual depictions of men for the earlier part of our period due to the relative lack of Cherokee women's images in the accessible record. There are several high-profile examples of Cherokee men choosing to wear and be depicted in the most up-to-date Euro-American fashions. In fact, "there was considerable variation in Cherokee men's attire- ranging from the newly fashionable suits with long pants worn by Europeans and Americans to calico frocks…similar in construction to outer-garments worn by American frontiersman [sic]" (Baker et al., 2018, p. 20).

We'd like to note that this cultural exchange in styles of dress went both ways, even as far north as the Colony of Maryland. Lisa recounts:

I visited Maryland's Fort Frederick Park for the first time in November of 2017, curious to "Discover the tale of the Cherokee Indians who worked with Maryland forces to defeat the French and their allies, the Shawnee and Delaware" (Maryland Department of Natural Resources, 2017). I brought some close friends along with me in case their planned special event on the Cherokee involvement with the Maryland colony in the French and Indian War was upsetting or dismissive. I was excited to meet whoever was giving this talk. I was amused that the day's interpreter was an England-born park ranger named Matthew due to scheduling issues with their usual expert. He was visibly concerned he would mispronounce the Cherokee names in his script. To my delight, the hour-long presentation was respectful of the Cherokee as knowledgeable and effective allies, describing the context around the spring of 1757, in which, "a Cherokee war party made its way north from the Cherokee towns" (Ware, 2023, p. 61). The speaker credited the direct influence of Cherokee men on changes to the official militia uniform in the late 1750s. The only statement that made me smile was the assertion that the calico cloth desired by the Cherokee men was "for their wives" as a kind of business trip gift. "Men wouldn't need to look pretty!" he editorialized, clearly lacking any understanding of Cherokee men's gender roles and interest in personal beauty.

Back to images of real, specific Cherokee men, who almost certainly wanted to look their best.

At first the famous 1828 lithograph of Sequoyah appears to show a man dressed very casually in a relatively unstructured garment cut like a twentieth century style bathrobe (Smithsonian National Portrait Gallery, *Sequoyah c. 1770–c. 1843*) [Fig. 2.2]. It's *not* a bathrobe, but it's also not quite the calico frock or the hunting shirt often worn by (or simply depicted on) American adventuring men like Davy Crockett. A closer look at his garments

Fig. 2.2 Sequoyah: National Portrait Gallery, Smithsonian Institution. Creative commons.

reveals a man seeking to represent himself as a gentleman scholar, much like David Rittenhouse when sitting for his portrait in Philadelphia in 1796 (Smithsonian National Portrait Gallery, David Rittenhouse). Sequoyah's shirt collar is starched and spotless, his cravat is carefully arranged, and his dark blue waistcoat has a wide, fashionably cut shawl collar. His outer garment is cut simply and appears to cover his body at least to his knees, with no standing collar. Like many authors in this era, he holds and points to a copy of his written work. In the context of the 1820s, such loose garments had intellectual associations, worn by many European men instead of a tailored coat. "Men's Indian [referencing India] gowns and banyans…ascribed elegance, creative ability and/or intellectual seriousness to their wearers" (North, 2020, p. 49). A similar men's gown is in the Mary D. Doering collection (Daughters of the American Revolution, 2016, p. 112).

Chief John Ross's depiction from 1843 [based on a painting made in 1835 according to James Mooney (Mooney, 2009, p. 150)] presents a man formally dressed as a politician prepared to sit down and negotiate with other world leaders. He wears a black coat, a figured waistcoat, and a black stock over a white shirt with fine gathers at the breast (Fig. 2.3). The cut of his coat and even the arrangement of his stock appear to be nearly identical to the garments worn by Mr. John Quincy Adams as captured by a series of daguerreotype portraits in 1843 (Smithsonian National Portrait Gallery, John Quincy Adams). Rather than catering to the colonizer's eye, John Ross may have been a distressing figure because "white Americans…expected their Indians to sport a Mohawk, wear earrings, and pick up a tomahawk when angry. By contrast, Ross, dressed neatly in a waistcoat, tail-coat, and bow

Fig. 2.3 John Ross: Smithsonian American Art Museum, Museum purchase. Creative commons.

tie, waged what this fellow Cherokee John Ridge called 'intellectual warfare'" (Saunt, 2020, p. 160). Chief Ross' finely tailored coat and coiffed hair represented resistance to Euro-American norms because "the success of the Cherokees in the White-dominated culture of the South was almost an insult" (Justice, 2006, p. 74).

Meanwhile,

> "many more [Cherokee] men wore calico frocks. Over their striped, floral, paisley, or gingham calico frocks, they invariably wrapped their upper bodies in finger-woven bandoliers and sashes, and their calves with finger-woven garters over their red wool leggings... donning traditional and ancient finger-woven male regalia, defined the calico frocks they wore within their own cultures' repertoire of signs...their lives were interlocked with Americans through cotton" (Baker et al., 2018, pp. 27–29).

Even the most Cherokee-coded garments were made from European-American materials by the early nineteenth century.

There are many examples in a surviving image of the International Indian Council photographed and then painted in 1843. Many of the Cherokee men attending may have wanted to assert their nationality through their clothing by wearing cotton frocks (Fig. 2.4). This boxy, caped garment has become a part of the cultural dress of modern Cherokee men, often donned when emphasizing cultural coherence, most notably in recent decades by Principal Chief Chadwick Smith (Fitzgerald, 2002, p. 81).

Just at the edge of this painting, we found a little group of women who we presume to be Cherokee or citizens of one of the other Nations at the Council. Two of the women wear white caps and 1840s hairstyles similar to the ones worn in

Cherokee culture in the nineteenth century   57

Fig. 2.4 John Mix Stanley, International Indian Council (Held at Tallequah, Indian Territory in 1843) Smithsonian American Art Museum. Creative commons.

the cased photograph collection of the Library Company of Philadelphia, such as their "Portrait of an unidentified, older woman, wearing a white cap, looking slightly to her right" (Accession number 8421.F.2). One bare-headed woman is wearing a striped or deeply pleated gown with a full skirt and a high, white collar. She's obscured and almost out of frame, but she's there.

In 1844, the "Cherokee Advocate newspaper began publication…subsidized by the nation…it appeared every two weeks and was bilingual…the advertisements of the local merchants in the paper indicated that there were people sufficiently well-off to purchase the latest fashions in clothing…from the East" (McLoughlin, 1993, pp. 80–81).

The Yale-educated Oswald Woodford arrived in the rebuilt Cherokee Nation in 1851 and reported that, "their homes… were similar in every way to the homes in Avon, Connecticut. The Cherokee read the same secular and religious newspapers that he read at home…[and] dressed as whites" (McLoughlin, 1984, pp. 479–480). His impression is borne out by the surviving images of the Cherokee family composed of George, Amanda, and Minerva Murrell: they are dressed and coiffed in the very latest 1850s fashions (Oklahoma Historical Society, 2024a)).

"Colonel Ethan Allen Hitchcock, an army officer who inspected the Indian country for the U.S. government," reported that, "[Lewis Ross] sold…some ready-made clothing, especially pantaloons and overcoats, and a great many shoes" (Perdue, 1979, p. 102).

By 1855, the principal of the Cherokee Female Seminary at Park Hill was photographed with two of her students in beautifully fitted and sewn dresses that are almost certainly worn over a full set of mid-nineteenth century-style petticoats based on how the garments fit and then skim the women's bodies (McLoughlin, 1984, p. 299).

If they generally took up the practice of corsetry, individual Cherokee women joined the women of England, Italy, Madagascar, and Mumbai (Gibson, 2020, p. 194).

Cherokee people weren't just consumers and wearers of European-style textiles. They made them, from fiber cultivation to finished garments. During treaty negotiations in 1785, the Cherokee negotiators stated that, "some of their women had lately learned to spin, and many others were 'very desirous that some method could be fallen on to teach them to raise flax, cotton, and wool, as well as to spin and weave it'" (Powell, 1887, p. 373).

This was specifically recommended by George Washington in 1796, when he wrote to us, "you should raise cotton, or flax, and have your wives and daughters taught to spin it up into thread, and weave it into cloth…" (Miles, 2015b, p. 35).

> "Women seized the opportunity to manufacture their own clothes…spinning, weaving and sewing conformed to women's practice of making clothing…and it promised to free them from dependence on the declining deerskin trade. Morovian missionaries who visited the Cherokees in 1799 reported that Cherokee women were so eager to make cloth that they carried spinning wheels on their backs from the agency to their homes" (Perdue, 1998, p. 117).

Spinning wheels aren't a weaving tool, but they speed up the hand production of thread and yarn considerably. "Throughout most of human history, producing enough yarn to make cloth was so time-consuming that this essential raw material was always in short supply" (Postrel, 2020, p. 43). Before the invention of the spinning jenny, "to supply a single weaver with yarn required twenty spinners" in the heart of England's Cheshire countryside (Postrel, 2020, p. 61). Modern spinners using a standard spinning wheel can expect to spend about 65 hours spinning the yarn for the warp and weft to weave a cloak for an average-height adult American woman. (Amos, 2001, pp. 249–254).

Cherokee women's skills in handling the materials and dyes for precontact clothing production may have positioned them well for taking up European-style spinning, weaving, and sewing once the new materials were available. Cherokee people had a strong tradition of using both bast fibers and fiber from various animals to produce garments and intricately decorated bandolier bags before the introduction of European textiles (Baker et al., 2018, p. 20). Before the arrival of European settlers, Cherokee women made their clothing from a range of materials, "including buffalo hair they collected after the animals had shed, which they wove into garments and pouches. Deerskins as well as fabrics made of hemp and mulberry bark were sewn into clothing with bone needles and thread of sinew" (Perdue, 1998, p. 22). In case your mental image of bison places them firmly in the prairies west of the Mississippi: bison were reported in Georgia into the early nineteenth century (National Park Service, 2016). These bison would have been the same species now raised for commercial meat, hide, and fiber by companies like The Buffalo Wool Company, who report yields of 4–6 ounces of spinnable fiber per animal, per annual shed (www.thebuffalowoolco.com).

Lisa has worked with shed bison down as a hand spinner. She reports that the end result is a beautiful, medium-brown yarn that can be as soft, fine, and warm as cashmere. Removing the guard hairs to prepare the fiber to spin by hand is labor intensive and requires delicate skill to produce yarn. The raw product is often full of dust or debris and lacks the relatively long, crimped fibers that give many sheep's wools some built-in coherence. In fact, a relaxed grip is needed to effectively spin bison down. This technique is known among modern spinners as long draw. It is very helpful in hand spinning cotton using either a drop spindle or a spinning wheel.

Cherokee women's interest and access to European-style textiles feature in an early story of trade in people.

> "As early as 1716, a Cherokee purchased from his captors a Frenchman taken in battle…he then apparently gave the Frenchman to his sister as she took him to Charles Town and sold him…in addition to being reimbursed in strouds…she received a suite of Calicoe Cloaths for herself and a suit of stuff and a hat for her son" (Reid, 2006, p. 130).

Nancy Ward nee Nanye'hi has a complex legacy well beyond the scope of this book. In her letter to the Cherokee people in 1817, she wrote, "Therefore children don't part with any more of our lands, but continue on it and enlarge your farms and cultivate and raise corn and cotton and we your mothers and sisters will make clothing for you…" (Carney, 2005, p. 38). This reads to us as an invitation to Cherokee men into the traditionally feminine space of agriculture in the context of the collapse of the buckskin economy. Virginia Moore Carney notes that Nancy's words reflect a worldview in which "their women can sew and spin in the fashion of white women, without sacrificing the essence of who they are" (p. 39). This may also have been an acknowledgment of the general value of women's textile production among their Euro-American peers. In the United States of the early nineteenth century, "textiles [were] more liquid than banknotes…In rural areas, women regularly paid for store goods with spinning or weaving" (Edwards, 2022, p. 127).

She was also reflecting changes that had already begun in the region's agriculture, partially driven by the theft of a "new" cotton variety from Mexico by the American adventurer Walter Burling before 1810 (Postrel, 2020, p. 22). This variety "ripened early… the bolls all appeared at about the same time…yielding about a third more usable cotton after ginning" (Postrel, 2020, p. 22).

> "Cotton itself was not a new crop – two of the fifty known species are native to the Americas – but…cultivation on the mainland was limited. Sea Island or long-staple cotton, so named for its long and silky fibers, grew along the coast and islands of South Carolina and Georgia, but it grew slowly and produced a relatively low yield. Separating the seeds from the fiber, a process called ginning, was also difficult…Short-staple cotton, which could be cultivated across a broader inland region, was…harder to gin because the seeds had a furry, green coating that clung to the fiber" (Rogers, 2010, p. 43).

Planters allowed the new cotton variety to cross-pollinate with the common Georgia Green Seed variety, which led to further improvements in cotton yield (Postrel, 2020, pp. 22–23).

By the mid-1810s, Cherokee people were described by the superintendent of Indian Trade as excelling in agriculture and wearing homespun clothing (Saunt, 2020, p. 23). The stage was originally set by the results of a negotiated treaty in 1791. In 1801, Hawkins reported that "we find the chiefs of the mountain towns complaining that the people of the [other] settlements had received more than their fair share of spinning wheels and cards, and were consequently more advanced in making their own clothing" (Mooney, 2009, p. 72).

The 1825 census taken by the Cherokee council was described in the *Cherokee Phoenix* as tallying up 2,428 spinning wheels and 769 looms (McLoughlin, 1984, p. 240). The 1835 American census-takers counted 2,484 weavers and 3,129 spinners in a population dwelling in 8,184 houses (McLoughlin, 1984, p. 241).

> "Cherokee freedwoman Eliza Whitmore…[who] migrated to Indian Territory as a young girl, recalled enslaved women's work of spinning and weaving. Whitmore described how enslaved African Indian women's position in antebellum Indian Territory translated into their role as conduits of some knowledge to Indian women…'every farm home…or most of them owned an old time spinning wheel…many an old Indian woman…learned the art and did this for themselves and their entire family, after we were set free'" (Naylor, 2008, pp. 94–95).

> "In many ways cotton *was* the Industrial Revolution. Grown around the world, cotton was typically shipped to Great Britain, where it was cleaned and carded, drawn, roved, spun, and finally woven into textiles. It was an industry worth millions to the British, even in the day of small-scale production methods. The advent of industrialization in the middle of the eighteenth century… made the manufacture of textiles cheaper and faster, fueling a global demand for cotton goods and thereby increasing the value of the raw staple many times over" (Rogers, 2010, pp. 43–44).

> "Gins had been around for centuries, but it was Eli Whitney's wire-toothed fin, patented in 1794, that made cotton a cash crop in America…In one day Whitney's gin did the work of two thousand men, and this meant that more – much more – cotton could be planted…

but picking cotton still had to be done by hand because it took strength and dexterity to pull the fiber from the boll without damaging the plant. It also took practice… the field hands – known by the part of their body worth the most to planters – had to pick with care or face a whipping" (Rogers, 2010, pp. 44–45).

Cotton fabric, and the skills to raise, prepare, work, and wear it, was not part of an overall "civilizing" of Cherokee people, but must be understood in the context of our own traditions of adaptability, curiosity, and enduring interest in education. Our ancestors apparently leveraged their existing kinship and economic relationships to enjoy the hygienic and aesthetic benefits of appropriate clothes in a world where they had no air conditioning, sunscreen, or indoor plumbing, all later innovations that have made the relative comfort of multiple petticoats supported with a corset nearly invisible to twenty-first-century people.

A history of photography and self-presentation in Indian Territory

We do not have a photograph of Polly, although it wouldn't be impossible that one existed. The rights and equipment needed to create daguerreotypes arrived in the United States in 1839. "Within two or three years, studios were common even in small towns, with practitioners moving west with the earliest settlers" (Severa, 1995, p. 1). Molly Rogers notes that "The daguerreotype quickly became a global phenomenon but enjoyed its greatest popularity in America, with more images made in the United States than anywhere else…By 1850 more than three million images were made annually in the United States" (2010, pp. 10–11).

Making a daguerreotype is not a quick process. First, a copper plate must be "cleaned, polished, and coated in silver." The silver is turned into light-sensitive silver iodide by being placed in a box with vapor of iodine. The prepared plate goes into a slide, which is attached to the back of the camera. After exposure, the plate is taken into a workroom where heated mercury fumes develop the image. This chemical process is stopped by washing the plate in hyposulfite of soda. The finished plate is then dried, covered in glass, and placed in a case to protect it (Rogers, 2010, pp. 224–225).

What did these photographs mean to the people who appeared in them, made them, and looked at them?

> "From the start photography was many things at once, and so it did not lend itself to meaning that was necessarily stable or shared. Photography was a chemical science and a fine art, a kind of magic or conjuring trick, as well as an industry and a craft. A single photograph was a representation and a two-dimensional image; it could 'immortalize' a person, object, or scene and also make something or someone appear quite dead" (Rogers, 2010, p. 14).

Nearly three decades before Polly's death, in the summer of 1843, delegates at a conference convened by John Ross in Tahlequah, the capital of the Cherokee Nation, posed for daguerreotypes and sketches by John Mix Stanley and Caleb Sumner Dickerman. Ross's brother, Lewis Ross, also invited the portrait artists to his home, where over the next few days, ten daguerreotypes were made (Sandweiss, 2002, pp. 209–210). The daguerreotypes have all been lost, although John Mix Stanley's painting is in the Smithsonian American Art Museum. (Smithsonian American Art Museum).

The resulting oil painting titled, "International Indian Council (Held at Tallequah, Indian Territory, in 1843) (Fig. 2.4)," is 40 inches by 31 inches. The subject is a packed pavilion with open sides. The image is partially dominated by a dark, wooden roof. Most of the people in the image are men, although some women are barely in frame: two of them wear white caps partially covering their hair. The delegates' clothing shows a wide range of fashion: everything from breechcloths to black suits with neckties. One participant has a top hat and a very committed mustache. Everyone's clothing is depicted as red, white, black, or blue. Many of the men wear Cherokee-style turbans. Two men, central to the composition, look right at the viewer: one in a military-style suit and, just to his left, the other wearing large earrings, a long shirt with full sleeves, a turban, and either a shawl or a matchcoat. The military man has been identified by the Smithsonian as Zachary Taylor (Smithsonian American Art Museum, Object number 1985.66.248,934B). No one else is named, but we must assume that the delegates from the Cherokee Nation and other tribes chose their clothing with deliberate care.

It is not a stretch to say that photographs of Native Americans served an important role in the development of propaganda and mythmaking in the American West.

"The U.S. Government used photography to further its policies. Photographs from the geological surveys and other expeditions, including pictures of western tribes, were widely published, exhibited and sold. In addition, the government commissioned portraits of Indian delegations that visited Washington, D. C., usually to sign treaties giving up their land. These pictures depicted the Indians as tame and harmless, suggesting that the 'Indian Problem' was under control. If the Indians came to Washington dressed in suits and ties, as they often did, the photographers kept a supply of traditional buckskins and feathered headdresses in their studios. Individuals and groups were posed for portraits in ceremonial dress, usually holding a tomahawk or peace pipe. The photographs needed to fit the prevailing stereotypes" (Clee, 2003, p. 67).

There is a persistent myth, even today, that Native Americans were universally superstitious, or at least suspicious, about photography. Hesitation or refusal of photography could be seen, instead, as a resolve to gain control, quite literally, over one's own image.

Daguerreotypes are difficult to make and are also not the easiest things in the world to see. They must be "held in one's hands at just the right angle to avoid the distraction of reflected light." As such, they could be considered "intrinsically private" (Sandweiss, 2002, p. 33). In the late 1850s, photographic processes that used a negative, in contrast to the positive-only production of a daguerreotype, allowed for mass production of photographic images. This ability to make multiple copies of a single image opened up the market for photographs as commercial commodities. Photographs and, to a certain degree, the people depicted within those photographs, were available for public consumption in a way never seen before (Sandweiss, 2002, pp. 216–217).

> "As the native subjects of the portraits lost control over the physical objects themselves, they also lost control over the stories that the pictures would be used to tell… the vast majority of photographs of Indian subjects came to serve the needs of their non-Indian makers and publishers. And most quickly found their place within a single overarching narrative story…the determinist tale of a 'vanishing race.'…The romantic primitivism and imagined antimodernism embedded in the vanishing race ideology is largely responsible for the widespread cultural assumptions about Indian fears of photographic technologies" (Sandweiss, 2002, pp. 217–219).

American critic Susan Sontag, writing in the 1970s, illuminated the tension between photography, tourism, and Native American reality rather succinctly.

> "The predatory side of photography is at the heart of the alliance, evident earlier in the United States than anywhere else, between photography and tourism. After the opening of the West in 1869 by the completion of the transcontinental railroad came the colonization through photography. The case of the…(Native Americans) …is the most brutal. Discreet, serious amateurs like (Adam Clark) Vroman had been operating since the end of the Civil War. They were the vanguard for an art of tourists

who arrived by the end of the century, eager for 'a good shot' of Indian life. The tourists invaded the Indians' privacy, photographing holy objects and the sacred dances and places, if necessary paying the Indians to post and getting them to revise their ceremonies to provide more photogenic material…The photographer both loots and preserves, denounces and consecrates. Photography expresses the American impatience with reality, the taste for activities whose instrumentality is a machine" (1977, pp. 64–65).

Despite this onslaught, resistance was possible and practiced. Modern readers might be surprised to learn of the level of sophistication some famous Native Americans had toward the commercialization of their images. Sitting Bull, for example, stipulated in his 1885 contract with Buffalo Bill's Wild West Show that he be the only person allowed to make money from souvenir pictures of himself, and he also charged a fee to pose in tintypes with patrons. In 1904, the Apache leader Geronimo sold his photos and autographs at the St. Louis World's Fair and left with "more money than he had ever before had in his life." A year later, he sat for Edward S. Curtis in a somber pose, looking off to the left, his clothing covered by a blanket, cloth wrapped around his head. A short time later, Geronimo published Geronimo's Story of His Own Life, which included a halftone reproduction of a photograph of him "Ready for Church" (Sandweiss, 2002, pp. 230–232). In this image, his short hair is neatly combed, and his suit jacket would not look out of place next to one in the 1902 edition of the Sears, Roebuck Catalogue (1969, p. 1132). A shirt very similar to his with a "tie to match that can be tied either in a knot or bow" is advertised for sale on page 961 of the same catalog. What appears, at first glance, to be a round amulet or necklace is actually a Dorset shirt button and would have been a bit old-fashioned at the time, but not anachronistic (Olski, 2022).

While being held by the US government, Geronimo may not have had much choice in the clothes he wore. But, even in the photos taken of him during his surrender in 1886 by Camillus S. Fly, he wears a white cloth shirt that comes down over the top of his breechcloth (Current, 1986, pp. 206–210).

The technology that allowed photography to come within the reach of ordinary people documenting their own lives wasn't developed until 1878, and snapshots, as we might think of them today, were essentially invented by George Eastman with the introduction of the Kodak camera ten years later (Tagg, 2021, pp. 53–54).

Without photographs of Cherokee women from Polly's exact time and place, we are left to peer back as far in time as we are able. From the place that is now the State of Oklahoma, we have a remarkable body of work by Jennie Ross Cobb, a Cherokee woman who lived from 1881 to 1959 (Minneapolis Institute of Art, 2023, p. 104 and p. 168). Almost two dozen of her photographs from 1896 to 1906 are available online on the Oklahoma Historical Society's website (Oklahoma Historical Society, 2024b). Her subjects are dressed identically to their contemporaries in the United States at the same time. We leave it to the reader to compare the clothing in Cobb's 1902 "Ozark & Cherokee Central Railroad" (Oklahoma Historical Society (2024c) photograph with the records from the same year on the Library of Congress's blog post "Women's Fashion History Through Newspapers: 1900–1920," (Thomas, 2021) and with Charles Van Schaick's photographs from his small town of Black River Falls, Wisconsin, in 1900 (Severa, 1995, p. 538).

Jennie Ross Cobb's work provides a stark contrast to the efforts of a man whose photography has become perhaps the most well known of Native American life from the same time period. Edward S. Curtis published his life's work, The North American Indian, in twenty volumes from 1907 to 1930. The collection was partially financed by J. P. Morgan and included over 2,200 photographs representing more than 80 North American tribes (Clee, 2003, pp. 79–81).

Curtis's work is objectively beautiful, but modern viewers should always keep in mind that they were not objective records of fact. "Curtis is attacked most often, and most legitimately, for his lack of ethnographic veracity. His soft focus blurred what might have been important details" (Lippard, 1992, p. 25).

> "By his own admission, Curtis's purpose was to preserve the past…Curtis controlled his photographs more explicitly in ways that had become the stock and trade of many western photographers…Among Curtis's most popular pictures are portraits of Indian people in Traditional clothes – feather headdresses, buckskins, bead necklaces. Sometimes the captions for these photos suggest that this was everyday wear. The fact is that most Indians in the early twentieth century wore pretty much what other Americans were wearing. But an Indian in a suit or a pair of pants and cotton shirt would hardly have aroused feelings of a romantic past. If the right

clothing wasn't available, Curtis sometimes designed or supplied it himself, even providing wigs if his subjects had cut their hair. Curtis was also careful to avoid including modern articles in his portraits…And if an offending object had been accidentally included, it would be gone before the picture was printed. One negative, for example, shows that great care was taken to scratch out an alarm clock" (Clee, 2003, pp. 82–85).

Ironically,

"systematic efforts at deculturation and geographic dispossession were accompanied by interest in native women's crafts, as middle-class Victorians purchased needlework curios, ceramics, and blankets to decorate their parlors and gain access to the free and natural life that Native Americans had come to symbolize" (Simonsen, 2006, p. 184).

Images from this era often focus on the assumed exotic nature of the native sitter and on their beautiful, fashionable handwork, fully removed from the context of the culture those works represented.

Discerning color in early photography

Whether a black-and-white photographic image is made on a glass plate, tintype, or more modern-day film, an unavoidable loss of information takes place in the transition from the world in color to an image in shades of gray. Early manuals for the public included tips on how to pose and what to wear, as well as warnings not to wear the color blue, which appeared white in final images, or dark green, which looked black (Groom, 2012, p. 200).

> "While the images may seem to resemble today's black and white photographs, the viewer must avoid making misleading assumptions about color based on the shades in the photo. The effect of color on early photography was quite different then…an apparently light-colored object could be a dark blue, and a nearly black object could be a pale yellow" (Greene, 2014, p. 6).

We hope, by now, you have accepted our assertion that Cherokee culture and citizenship have nothing to do with skin tone or complexion, despite what some writers, even the influential Mooney, had to say about it in the nineteenth and twentieth centuries.

> "Much of the advance in civilization had been due to the intermarriage among them of white men, chiefly traders of the ante-Revolutionary period…Most of this white blood was of good stock, very different from the "[slur for Native women] man" element of the western tribes. Those of the mixed blood who could afford it usually sent their children away to be educated, while some built schoolhouses upon their own grounds and brought in private teachers from the outside. With the beginning of the present century we find influential mixed bloods in almost every town, and the civilized idea dominated even the national councils. The Middle towns, shut in from the outside world by high mountains, remained a stronghold of Cherokee conservatism" (Mooney, 1902, p. 84).

Let us add another layer to that: you can't assume from early photographs that you are looking at an accurate depiction of a person's complexion in the first place. The image of Harriet Tubman taken in the 1860s and displayed at the National Museum of African American History and Culture in 2019 is a wonderful example of this. Lonnie Bunch commented,

> "This new photograph shows her relaxed and very stylish. Sitting with her arm casually draped across the back of a parlor chair, she's wearing an elegant bodice and a full skirt with a fitted waist. Her posture and facial expression remind us that historical figures are far more complex than we realize" (National Museum of African American History and Culture., n.d.).

To the modern viewer, her skin looks relatively dark, nearly the same tone as her hair. Her blouse, which was probably red if it was the fashionable Garibaldi style, reads as very dark. Other, widely published photographs of her also appear to show a relatively dark complexion (National Geographic Kids., n.d.).

This is in contrast to how she was described by the people trying very hard to get help identifying and finding her in 1849. The advertisement placed in the Delaware Gazette by her enslavers described her as "chestnut colored" (Dupuis, 2022).

Lisa's experience with wet plate photography

By the spring of 2023, I had nearly completed my first 1830s ensemble. I wanted to celebrate the end of this multi-layered project, which dominated my sewing output for more than four months. I had read about the Victorian Photography Studio on the Redthreaded blog, and I wanted a wet plate taken. I needed dressing help and moral support, so I invited my friend, Naomi Doddington, to join me.

On May 20, 2023, I arrived in Gettysburg, VA, with a bale of finished garments in my car's trunk. It was a glorious, late spring day.

I have very light skin. My skin is so light that it usually takes a few tries to find a foundation that's pale enough to match me while still warm in tone. While I don't usually wear a full face of makeup, that day I ended up mixing two Too Faced brand foundations called "Snow" and "Pearl."

I thought I knew what my skin would look like in the tintype: pale. I had no idea what my eyes would look like. Blue eyes look very white in this process, while dark eyes look very black. But my eyes are hazel: a green with yellow rings around the pupil.

Compare for yourself: we've included reproductions of my tintype with a printed digital photograph of myself in the same light and clothes on the Twins N Needles instagram account.

Fig. 2.5 shows Lisa and Naomi in the tintype, and Fig. 2.6 shows them in an iPhone photo.

My bright red gown with blue flowers looks almost black with white flowers in the tintype. My turquoise earbobs look like they are made of white pearls. My skin reads as a medium tan, closer to the "nude" L'eggs hosiery color than it ever has been. My eyes look like tiny bull's eyes: the dark green in each iris reads as very pale, and the yellow bands are quite dark, so my pupils appear

Fig. 2.5 Naomi Doddington (left, seated) and Lisa Neel, Gettysburg, PA, May 20, 2023. Tintype by Victorian Photography Studio, image by Lara Neel.

Cherokee culture in the nineteenth century   77

Fig. 2.6 Lisa Neel (left) and Naomi Doddington, Washington, DC, July 20, 2024. Image taken by Naomi Doddington.

to be hugely dilated, and my irises' show up as faint shadows. In contrast, here's a close-up of me in the same ensemble, captured using modern digital photography (Fig. 2.7).

Fig. 2.7 Lisa with the same ensemble and bonnet on as in the tintype. Photo by Lara Neel.

In short, I unintentionally proved a point I didn't know I had: that people with reddish skin tones can look much darker in wet-plate photography than they are in life, regardless of their overall complexion. This observation explains why some images of Chief Ross from early in his life look relatively dark and later images look pale. He didn't necessarily become lighter as he aged; the technology capturing his face changed.

Conclusion: What did all this do to inform our depictions of Polly?

This helped us depict Polly as a woman living through a dynamic period of complex cultural change. Unable to work with direct images of her, we explored how other Cherokee women expressed their choices and adapted new technologies to their lives. We had to challenge the assumptions of nineteenth- and twentieth-century sources and strip away antique patinas of our beloved cultural costume.

Finally, we had to acknowledge the potential that she actively participated in enslavement with the certainty that she directly benefited from the enslavement of other humans for the bread on her table and money in her pocket.

3
Why it matters: Investigating the archives and embracing all legal Cherokees

"You can't judge the past by the present. It's a splendid slogan. It permits us to set aside the missteps of history and offers and covenant with the future, allowing us to be held blameless for the decisions we make today. Ignorance…Our grandparents didn't know any better. We didn't know any better. If we knew then what we know now, we wouldn't have done what we did" (King, 2013, p. 264).

"We didn't practice slavery. Our family was poor and fled during the Civil War." That's the story we heard as children in the mid-1990s, when Freedmen's rights were in the news due to the community debates following the "R.H. Nero v. Cherokee Nation" court case.

In the summer of 2018, Lara got curious about Polly's story. She doesn't remember how she found it, but she discovered pretty early on that Polly's family were enslavers. We dug into the National Archives and the Oklahoma Historical Society to find more details.

While we don't judge our grandparents and parents for giving us incorrect information about our family's enslavement of people, we felt our depiction of Polly Beck's context had to include it. Focusing exclusively on pretty calico dresses and the rustle of starched petticoats is a privilege left to Cherokee historians of the 1950s and 1960s, before the phenomenal work of Theda Perdue (1979), William G. McLoughlin (1984), and Tiya Miles (2010 and 2015) revealed the probable connection between such material wealth and human bondage.

The Cherokee Nation as an enslaving state

Sources assessing the commitment of Cherokee people to chattel-style enslavement often draw contradictory conclusions. This may be because many scholars conflate chattel slavery with large-scale plantations. For example, Stremlau notes:

> "Although many Cherokees were growing cotton and spinning cloth, only a minority adopted the system of agriculture that would be associated with this crop in the Old South…the Cherokees who [were enslavers] were those who were most directly and aggressively participating in the developing commercial market of the American South" (Stremlau, 2011, p. 29).

Some sources argue that enslavement was practiced by an elite, small group. Others describe widespread enslavement and armed defense of chattel slavery as an institution. Theda Perdue's influential work noted a possible spectrum informed by adaptation of White American lifeways: "In addition to the highly acculturated [enslavers]…a few conservative Cherokees [enslaved people] but they seem to have valued their [bondspeople] less for labor than for companionship and particularly for the ability to speak English" (Perdue, 1979, p. 106).

McLoughlin summarizes, "By 1835 there were 15,000 Cherokees and 1,592 [enslaved persons] …by the time of the Civil War… there were 17,000 Cherokees and 4,000 [enslaved persons]" (1984, p. 277). Indeed, "one did not have to touch or even be around enslaved people to benefit from their stolen labor" (McGill, Jr., and Frazier, 2023, p. 206).

It's tempting to compare Cherokee antebellum enslavement proportions to those of Americans. But the 75 percent of white families that didn't directly have paperwork linking them to people who were legally property still "participated in the institution of slavery and benefitted from the theft of labor" (Harriott, 2023, p. 335).

It's tempting to search for evidence that enslavers, the Cherokees "treated their [enslaved people] very leniently" (McLoughlin, 1984, p. 277). Some Cherokee families were dependent on their enslaved people's English-speaking skills and ordered them to become formally educated. "[Enslaved people] of Cherokees took on the role of translators and instructors in [mission schools] …

became indispensable in the education and religious instruction of their [enslavers]" (Miles, 2015b, p. 94).

Even during the removal,

> "[enslaved people] went ahead of the wagons with axes and cleared obstructions from the trail…acted as watchmen at night…hunted for game…and worked for [their enslavers] as teamsters, cooks, and nurses. The labor of [the enslaved] and the services that they performed spared slaveholders some of the suffering experienced by other Cherokees in the course of the removal" (Perdue, 1979, 71).

Tiya Miles further argues that,

> "the theft and destruction of lives, lands, and cultures link these [chattel enslavement and removal] as holocausts, and in the specific context of Cherokee history, slavery and removal are intimately connected. The expulsion of Cherokee people cleared the way for the expansion of American slavery…at the same time, the presence of [enslaved people] during removal made it possible for their Cherokee masters to survive the ordeal and to rebuild efficiently in the West" (Miles, 2015b, p. 153).

> "In addition to bearing the hardships of the journey, [enslaved people] were enlisted to do the additional work of hunting for their masters, nursing the sick, preparing meals, guarding the camps at night, and hiking ahead of the group to ensure passable roads" (Miles, 2015b, p. 155).

After removal, Cherokee leaders in Indian Territory

> "reinstated and strengthened the Eastern Cherokee slave code, once again outlawing Cherokee-black intermarriage and property ownership by [enslaved people]. The Cherokee rape law that had once included equal protection for all women and equal punishment for all men now distinguished between Cherokees and blacks…black male [enslaved people] could be put to death for rape- unless the victim was a black woman" (Miles, 2015b, pp. 166–167).

Tellingly, the Cherokee enslavers held on to their enforced labor force even after removal to the West made large cotton plantations unprofitable. "After removal planters grew cotton primarily for domestic consumption…many Cherokees raised sheep and made their clothing of wool or wool mixed with cotton rather than fabric woven from cotton alone" (Perdue, 1979, p. 99). " In the 1840's, the Cherokee Advocate newspaper frequently published letters from enslavers seeking to "recoup stolen [enslaved people] or to replace them" (Miles, 2015b, p. 167).

The link between the "story of the emergence of the Cherokee Nation from post-removal in 1839 to the golden age of recovery and prosperity prior to and after the U.S. Civil War is one of tenacity and interminable faith" (Baker et al., 2018, p. 71). The Park Hill area of Cherokee Nation, near Tahlequah, was named by "Missionary Reverend Samuel Newton, because 'it resembled the estates of the noblemen in England'" (Baker et al., 2018, p. 34). It was also "home to the plantation class of Cherokee people, and this reality can hardly be ignored especially in discussion of the large, luxurious homes of individuals like George M. Murrell, John Ross, and his brother Lewis Ross" (Baker et al., 2018, p. 39). Surviving images of these stately homes lead the viewer to wonder if any brickwork might bear the fingerprints of the enslaved workers like the ones that Joseph McGill, Jr. describes in his writing on the Slave Dwelling Project.

As Tiya Miles observed, "Comparing degrees of enslavement seems a hollow and even barbaric exercise, but it is one that former slaves themselves found it necessary to engage in" (2015b, p. 43). Some enslavers left evidence of a self-conscious awareness of degrees of barbarism. Peter Hildebrand, our grandfather's great-grandfather's uncle, born in the 1780s according to family records, placed an advertisement seeking the return of Allen, who had self-liberated in September of 1845.

> "In his advertisement, Hildebrand offered no explanation for Allen's departure, only a brief description of Allen's physical characteristics…As Hildebrand explained defensively, Allen had 'marks of the whip, inflicted before he came into my possession.' Hildebrand insinuated that he was not the kind of [enslaver] who would whip enslaved people…it was important to him to describe himself in a certain way- as the kind of righteous [enslaver] William Potter Ross promoted in his *Cherokee Advocate* editorial" (Naylor, 2008, p. 40).

It's the enslaver's version of putting lipstick on a pig, hinting at the threat of violence that kept "good" enslavers in business. Yes, we're calling our ancestor a ᏏᏆ (se-qua). We're not sorry.

We reject any rosy view in light of consistent resistance to enslavement exhibited by many people held in bondage by Cherokee enslavers. Happy members of the family do not seek to change their circumstances through "harsh words, subtle deeds, forceful threats…suicide…and attempted escapes" (Miles, 2010, p. 95).

Individual Cherokee families determined for themselves how directly they participated in enslavement. Then the American Civil War arrived in Indian Territory.

> "The Civil War split the Cherokee Nation along a rift that had opened before Removal…when the Cherokee Confederate and Union regiments were formed, the divide was not between slaveholding mixed-bloods on one side and antislavery full bloods on the other. Rather, the split was between the Ross Party [Unionists] and the Treaty-Old Settler Party [Cherokee Nationalist Confederates]" (Parins, 2003, p. 193).

Chief John Ross' attempts to maintain Cherokee neutrality fell apart in 1861, when a council was held that "about four thousand Cherokee males attended" (Conley, 2005, p. 174). Whether Cherokee Nation as a state was actually neutral, Confederate, or Union in the conflict of the United States Civil War is too big of a topic for a pair of independent fashion historians to fully untangle, so we'll leave it at this: whether you could consistently draw a clear line distinguishing abolitionist and pro-enslavement Cherokee citizens before the organization of the Knights of the Golden Circle and the Keetoowah secret societies (Miles, 2015b, p. 186), the sheer number of Cherokee Freedmen who managed the bureaucratic, high-scrutiny process to enroll as citizens during the Dawes Commission's work suggests that a significant population was held in bondage in Cherokee Nation by the early 1860s.

"In the end [of the Dawes process] there were 14,798 enrolled citizens, of whom 4,924 were freedpeople" (Naylor, 2008, p. 181).

The Dawes Commission defined legal Cherokees

"With the Confederate defeat came a Cherokee defeat that would deepen Cherokee subjugation to the federal government. The Cherokees had been the first of the Five Tribes to free their [enslaved people] in 1863, but the Treaty of 1866…forced the Cherokee to go one step further and accept these former [enslaved people] as full citizens" (Miles, 2015b, p. 188).

Modern Cherokee citizenship includes the descendants of the formerly enslaved as described by the terms in two treaties. The 1865 and 1866 treaty terms set boundaries on the Freedmen's inclusion and made specific space for them in the Cherokee reservation.

"At length the United States Commissioners, despairing of success with the loyal element [Union allies], concluded a treaty with the Southern party [On June 13, 1865]. Among other things, this treaty provided that a quantity of land equal to 160 acres for every man, woman, and child, including the freedmen belonging to the Southern party…should be set apart…for their sole use and occupancy" (Powell, 1887, p. 346).

A further treaty was signed on July 19, 1866.

> "The fourth article…contained a provision setting apart a tract within the Cherokee country known as the Canadian district, for the settlement and occupancy of 'all the Cherokees and freed persons who were formerly [enslaved by] any Cherokee, and all free [people] not having been [enslaved] who resided in the Cherokee Nation prior to June 1, 1861" (Powell, 1887, p. 369).

Further, the ninth article included,

> "all freedmen who had been liberated by voluntary act of their former [enslavers] or by law, as well as all free [African-descended] persons who were in the country at the commencement of the rebellion and were still residents therein or who should return within six months and their descendants, should have all the rights of native Cherokees" (Powell. 1887, p. 370).

Bear in mind that land was still held in common by the tribe. This treaty did not provide allotments to freed people and their children; it set aside a place for them to live and gave them citizenship.

Allotment occurred later, in the Dawes Commission process, which created a closed set of legal Cherokees, including three groups: Cherokees by blood, Cherokees by marriage, and Cherokee Freedmen.

In a show of grit and determination, former bond people and their children traveled to report to the Dawes Commission 35 years after emancipation, gathered documents, gave testimony, and assembled friends and former neighbors to support their claims to identity. The typed depositions reflect rushed, impersonal questioning and deserve more study.

For any Cherokee, tracing their ancestry back to the Dawes rolls is now a routine part of the enrollment process. The Dawes Commission is now so far in the past that records that may have caused considerable distress when they were taken are now cherished documents for many. It's now significant for a Cherokee person to handle their ancestor's Dawes record and learn how to find their card number. Interacting with the Freedman rolls to find the people our family enslaved felt transgressive and uncomfortable. But it also suggested a moderate measure of initial equity in the form of access to land allotments as Cherokee citizens.

As Marilyn Vann testified in 2022:

> "[during the early 20th century] Each tribe signed an allotment agreement which detailed the size of the allotments and other criteria such as cut off days to apply for allotments for their citizens…Freedmen of the Cherokee, Creek, and Seminole tribes received the same size land allotments as by blood members of the tribe (Senate Committee on Indian Affairs)."

It's a small comfort, but we do find it satisfying that the Cherokee Nation agreed to honor the citizenship of the Freedmen during the difficult Allotment period of our history.

Publicly acknowledging specific oppressions

The connections between Freedmen and the people who held them in violent bondage aren't made obvious by most of the roll sources in use today. We had to dig into archives to develop a clear-eyed, truthful understanding of our family's practice of enslavement and probable armed defense of it. If an index linking enslavers or specific work sites to the Freedmen rolls has been made, we haven't found it. There is no well-documented community list for the Beck-Hildebrand mill such as the one Tiya Miles compiled for the Diamond Hill work camp (Miles, 2006, pp. 219–231). When we found some of these records, we originally thought they were our direct relations because some Freedmen kept their enslavers' family names as their legal names: Beck, Hildebrand, and Ward. Reading the records themselves quickly disabused us of this hope and revealed distressing, person-specific links to enslavement.

Despite the bland horror of a mass-printed Federal form collecting information on human beings in the reconstruction era with an entry space for "Owner's Name," reviewing enrollment applications bears fascinating hints of the person's life story. Each record has at least one deposition, carefully typed, and at least one form filled out in the rolling, professional hand of a Federal clerk in the time before ballpoint pens were widely available. The commissioners have an agenda and voice their opinions, at turns scolding, judging, and questioning the applicants.

We hope these records receive more scholarly attention in the future. They're rich, interesting, and important documents.

We decided to include a public discussion of the evidence we found of our family's enslavement of specific people alongside the lighthearted "Get Dressed with Me" and "How much does it cost to dress Polly?" videos. We wanted to bring the humans who were involuntarily connected to our family into the full context while being careful not to exploit their stories. This felt especially important in 2023, with the uptick in media interest in the Tulsa Race Massacre, including a moving depiction in the fictionalized Tulsa, Oklahoma, of the television show *Lovecraft Country* (National Public Radio, 2021) and commemorations by the United States Commission on Civil Rights. (2021)

We wrote up a script, analyzing some of the archival material from the Dawes Commission's work to enroll Freedmen. Then, we reached out to a person we trusted to advise us and edit our work: Nuova Wright.

We first met Nuova in a summer creative writing class in the early 1990s. Always gracious with the use of their time and intelligence, Nuova is also a wonderful poet and has been a steadfast friend throughout our lives.

Nuova encouraged us to develop a companion video, specifically on "How to Search for Your Dawes Enrollee," informing us of the relative invisibility of the Dawes Commission's work to the general population.

The survivor Rachel Ward

We began by comparing the Dawes Commission enrollment packets of Julia Ann Bee (Polly's daughter, our grandfather's grandmother) and Rachel Ward as a case study comparing the experiences of two women who grew up on the same land, breathed the same air, and routinely experienced the churning clatter of the mill. They had equal rights to Cherokee citizenship in 1901, yet faced wildly different burdens of proof as the Dawes Commission performed their work.

My first indication that access to these records remains informally segregated was the response I got from the Oklahoma Historical Society when I requested copies of her packet:

> "We have received your request for 3 Dawes Packets and will process it as soon as payment is received. I'm only charging you for 2 because Willnora C.J. Bee and Julia A. Bee are on the same packet. *I also want to let you know that Rachel Ward is on the roll as a Cherokee Freedman.* If payment is not received within 2 weeks, we will assume you are no longer interested in the information." [Emphasis mine] (Oklahoma Historical Society, 2022).

As previously described, Julia Ann's record is fairly standard for a Cherokee citizenship application without any complications or significant questioning, despite reflecting a long childbearing career with a series of husbands while living as the head of her own household. The Commissioners were able to find her name on previous census lists and noted the name changes she made over four marriages. They didn't closely question the paternity of her children, apparently relying on her testimony alone, supported by previous census records, to include her children as citizens. They didn't ask for exact dates of marriages or seek any proof from officiants or midwives.

In comparison to Julia Ann, we have more documentation about Rachel Ward because she was interviewed in the [*Work Projects Administration*] *Oklahoma Slave Narratives* and the Dawes Commission interrogated her much more about her life story. In the book edited by Lindsay Baker & Julie P. Baker (1996) on the narratives (pp. 445–449), she was interviewed at age 91, and her name was recorded as Rochelle Allred Ward. Living in Fort Gibson, Oklahoma, she included recollections about the Hildebrand mill in her narrative, which is how we first found her.

Her testimony outlined her parents' love story and how they navigated the desires of their enslavers to allow them to marry and build a life together. Further, she described how her father changed his last name to Beck after her mother, Lottie, convinced Joe Beck to buy him from a woman named Sarah Eaton. From this testimony, we get a sense of her large family: Her parents had at least seven children aside from Rachel: Sabra, Celia, Milton, Louie, Sam, Nelson, and Dennis.

Her Dawes enrollment packet (National Archives Catalog. Dawes Enrollment Jacket for Cherokee, Cherokee Freedmen, Card #294) is relatively slim compared to the other Freedmen's applications we reviewed, but it's much longer than Julia Ann's at 15 pages. We only looked at about 20 Freedmen's records, but by and large they were more than 8 pages long.

Children who enrolled with their mother are included on the front of her card with their father noted on the back. The card wasn't completed in a single snapshot of time like a census: children were added as they were born if they were born during the Commission's work. The ages given are the ages they were when they were enrolled.

Rachel lists herself as Cherokee "by adoption" in some documents, which is how some people were describing Freedman enrollment at that time. We have more details about her children and their fathers than we get out of Polly's record because the Commission more aggressively questioned her personal history.

Person first named: Rachel Ward, 38 years old, female

Dawes enrollment number 775.

Her father was James Beck, died before 1880, enrolled in Tahlequah, [Enslaver]: Joe Beck

Her mother was Lottie Beck, died before 1880, enrolled in Tahlequah, [Enslaver]: Joe Beck

Her children:

> 776. William Aldrich, 19 years old, male
> - Father: Amos Aldrich, "noncitizen"
> - Birthdate: March 19, 1882
>
> 777. Jesse Aldrich, 16 years old, male
> - Father: Amos Aldrich, "noncitizen"
>
> 778. Lewis Aldrich, 15 years old, male
> - Father: Amos Aldrich, "noncitizen"
>
> 779. Cora Ward, 4 years old, female
> - Father: Nelson Ward, "noncitizen" (on the card it says he's "noncitizen" but in her 1901 testimony she says he's a Cherokee citizen 'by adoption,' and also a US citizen)
> - Birthdate: April 30, 1897
> - Midwife: Dina Walker.
>
> 780. Dan Vann, 10 months old, male
> - Father: Jim Vann, Freedman/adoption
> - Birthdate: September 22, 1901
> - Midwife: Florence Narr (Naw?)

Note: The application for enrollment is specific that Rachel is "not the wife of Jim Vann," and her name is noted as Rachel Ward. It's hard to tell from the electronic copy of a scanned document, but it looks like the clerk had to do some scraping with a pen knife to get Ward out of the Vann he originally wrote.

In her 1930s testimony to the WPA, Rachel mentions having thirteen children in her life. She names Amos, Susie, Jess, Will, Frank, Lottie, and Cora.

Her enslaver Joe Beck

We think the Joe Beck who enslaved Rachel, her family, and several other families was probably both Julia Ann's maternal uncle and the father of Julia Ann's first husband (as we discussed earlier, records describe him under at least four names: Jesse Surry Eaton Beck, Sut Beck, Blacksoot, or "Black Sut").

Joe isn't a very unusual name, but we could only find one Joe Beck alive at the correct time range who died in 1863. His mother's birth name was Susannah Buffington.

We found seven people in the "Eastern Cherokee Applications, August 29, 1906–May 26, 1909" who gave Susannah Beck nee Buffington or Susannah Eaton nee Buffington as their grandmother and listed Susannah's children. These were Julia A. Bee, Susannah Chandler, Sabra Beck, Ellis Eaton, Martin Sturdivant, Amanda Cherokee Scott, and Walter Eaton.

Susannah Chandler (Chandler, application 868) reported her birth name as "Susannah Beck, Jr." She was born in 1852 and would have been almost 20 when her aunt, who she names as "Mary Beck," died in February of 1872.

Living in Arkansas at the time of her application to the Commissioner of Indian Affairs, she gave her father's name as Joseph Beck in English, Cah-le-ska-wee in Cherokee. Born in Georgia, he lived in the Delaware District of the Cherokee Nation, Indian Territory, in 1851 and died August 8, 1863.

The list of uncles and aunts reported by these cousins largely agrees with each other and is supported by the family list in the work of Emmet Starr (p. 337). All of this convinces us that Joe Beck, married to Cynthia Downing, who died before 1864, was Polly Beck's full brother and therefore our ancestral uncle.

As Rachel reported, "all over this country was Beck families."

We encourage you to read Rachel's testimonies for yourself in her own words. She paints a relatively rosy picture of life enslaved at the farm surrounding the mill and of Cynthia specifically, possibly out of concern that otherwise her testimony wouldn't be recorded. Joseph McGill, Jr. has noted that "some black historians have shied away from using the WPA Works Progress Administration (WPA) narratives because they are tainted with the racist intent to stereotype the elderly informants as loyal to their former masters" (p. 192). On a positive note, her words ring with pride on her family's skilled labor and relationship-building.

We hear you saying, "Everyone has an uncle they dread seeing at family holidays. That doesn't mean Polly Beck directly benefited from violent enslavement." Originally, we wanted to hide behind that also. It's tempting to say, "Our tragic ancestor was just a simple miller's wife and we can't prove she personally participated in violently extracting labor from people who were systematically denied their humanity."

But Cherokee families did not function on a "nuclear" family model. The Dawes Commission's work was an *attempt to create* nuclear families "as a means to assimilate Indian people into the margins of American society" (Stremlau, 2011, p. 4).

We can't even hide from the family's engagement with enslavement by focusing on the women and pretending they had no choices in this situation. "Indeed, the Cherokee Nation enacted several laws in the nineteenth century in order to protect the property, including enslaved people, of Cherokee women who had married non-Cherokee men" (Naylor, 2008, p. 58).

The survivor Nancy Sheppard

Nancy Sheppard survived enslavement as a child and then fought for an allotment on which her family could potentially build generational wealth and have safety and security (National Archives Catalog. Dawes Enrollment Jacket for Cherokee, Cherokee Freedmen, Card #186).

Nancy Sheppard, Dawes Roll number 511, was 48 when she was entered into the Freedmen roll in 1901. That means she was born in 1853.

Her father was Jesse Hildebrand—dead in 1901, but noted as being from the Illinois District. Her mother was Hannah Hildebrand, also dead in 1901. They were all held in slavery by "Mike Hildebrand." Their citizenship is listed as "colored."

Nancy's husband was named Morris Sheppard. He's listed on her card as a noncitizen, but in her testimony she comments that he is a citizen "but his rights are disputed."

Morris has his own section of the WPA narratives (Baker and Baker, 1996, pp. 375–382). He gave his testimonies when he was 85, reflecting on events that had happened when he was a teenager, but he mentioned that Nancy was born in Tennessee and raised at "the mill."

Nancy Sheppard's children were:
Fannie Sheppard, daughter, age 18
Emma Sheppard, daughter, age 16
Annie Sheppard, daughter, age 14
Thomas Sheppard, son, age 12
Claud Sheppard, son, age 10

Fannie had a daughter named Willie M. Sheppard, who was born in 1902.

Willie's father was Anderson Penn, a US citizen "by adoption."

Fannie and Willie were not married. The form required some crossing out and amendments to note this.

Nancy Sheppard was the midwife for her own daughter in the birth of her granddaughter and gave her mark on the child's birth affidavit.

She claimed an allotment of land in the early 1900s, as well as allotments for her children and her grandbaby.

Her enslaver Michael Hildebrand

"Mike Hildebrand" is referenced in several Freedmen enrollment folders that we found.

Michael reportedly emigrated to Indian Territory about 1859 (United States Census 1860, Canadian District, Cherokee Nation, Indian Lands, Arkansas; Roll: M653_52; Page: 1187, #391; Family History Library Film: 803052). He died in January 1863 at North Fork in the Creek Nation (now Eufaula, OK) at about age 82.

His first wife, Nancy "Nannie" Martin Hildebrand, was the daughter of Col. Joseph Martin and Elizabeth Ward and the granddaughter of Nancy Ward. According to family oral history, he lived at Ocoee (now Polk County), Tennessee, before the removal, where he had a ferry, two mills, and a large farm. His house was where the Federal Road crossed the Ocoee River.

Nannie died in 1837. Micheal then married Lucy Absher, a white woman, in 1839. It's unclear whether she emigrated to Indian Territory when he did.

Micheal didn't emigrate to Indian Territory with his children Peter and Stephen. It appears he emigrated on his own about 20 years later, bringing Nancy Sheppard and possibly the rest of her family with him. Nancy would have been a young child. We don't know his motivations to move from Tennessee when he was already in his late 60s, but the timing matches with Morris' testimony that Nancy was born in Tennessee and raised at "the mill."

Hildebrand was still an uncommon family name in Indian Territory, and there aren't any other Michael Hildebrands in the family tree that fit the correct age and time frame to be the "Mike" mentioned on Nancy's enrollment card.

Michael was Polly's father-in-law, and Julia Ann's grandfather, which makes him our fifth great-grandfather. This makes Nancy Sheppard one of the people whose life was involuntarily linked with our family. We can't pay her back or make it right, but we decided to say her name, acknowledge her, and do what we could to help her descendants feel sincerely welcome among their fellow Cherokee citizens. People remembered remain a little alive, so we are intentionally remembering Nancy.

We Are Cherokee

On July 8, 2023, the Cherokee Nation Chief, Chuck Hoskin, Jr., posed for a Cherokee Phoenix photographer with five members of the Cherokee Freedmen Project Committee.

> "The exhibit, which opened in September 2022, examined the history of Black slavery in the Cherokee Nation and sought to broaden the understanding of the Cherokee Freedman experience. It included stories, histories, images and documents of Cherokee Freedmen, with original artwork by [Cherokee Nation] artists" (a). (Cherokee Phoenix, 2023a)

Acceptance and visibility of Cherokee Freedmen have increased since the 1990s. It's encouraging that this particular part of the unfinished work of Reconstruction is progressing.

4
How we "dressed" Polly to bring her into the picture

How would Polly have followed fashion?

To learn how Polly may have dressed throughout her life, we first must determine how she would have decided to dress. In other words, how closely could she have followed the most up-to-date American fashions at the time?

Over 90 percent of adult white Americans in 1840 could read and write (Beveridge, 2011). In his recent history of literacy in the Cherokee Nation from 1820 to 1906, James Parins reports,

> "One of the great pillars of Cherokee intellectual life was the Cherokee Nation's dedication to education for all its citizens…the Cherokee school system…created an ethos in which the written word became an important part of the mostly rural and largely agricultural Cherokee Nation" (Parins, 2003, p. 68).

Literacy in the Cherokee language was estimated at 90 percent only a few years after Sequoyah invented a script for it in 1821 (Saunt, 2020, p. 54). Before there were formal classes or coursebooks in Sequoyah's syllabary, it spread from person to person, primarily among Cherokee-only speakers (Parins, 2003, p. 32). The structure of the writing system, similar to Japanese hiragana, is such that any speaker of Cherokee can quickly learn how to read and write it (Case, 2012, p. 3). The Cherokee National Council took significant steps to include all Cherokee audiences in their publication of the Cherokee Phoenix, a newspaper launched in 1828, meant to be a "readable weekly resembling in nearly every way the newspapers published in the progressive white communities across the Union" (Parins, 2003, p. 53). In 1827, the Nation hired white printers, built a print house, ordered a custom press and fonts, and hired Elias Boudinot to serve as the editor (Parins, 2003, p. 54–55). "The amount of Cherokee-language content varied from issue to issue…even though the syllabary-based Cherokee took up less space than the alphabet-based English, significant Native content appeared" (Parins, 2003, p. 57).

Looking closely at records related to Polly's family, the 1835 census of her stepfather's household listed "two readers of English" in the family. The whole list is Surry Eaton: Six Cherokees, 5 quarterbloods, 5 [bondspeople], 1 white intermarriage, 1 farmer, 2 readers of English, 1 weaver, 2 spinsters (Foreman, 1971, p. 160).

Julia Ann's 1906 packet gives a name in Cherokee for herself (Quah-la-yuke) and for her father, Stephen Hildebrand (Cun-aga-yun), but not for her mother, who she lists as "Mary or Polly," born in Georgia (Eastern Cherokee Applications, Application No. 859, pp. 1–26). If Polly had a formal name in Cherokee, Julia Ann would have been motivated to include it to secure her share of the money appropriated for the Eastern Cherokee Indians by Congress on June 30, 1906 (National Archives Catalog. Eastern Cherokee Applications, August 29, 1906–May 26, 1909).

This is all a bit of a preamble to say that, like most people, Polly could have kept up with fashion by reading about it as well as seeing other people wearing it. Marna Jean Davis has shown that, with the exception of style changes to make a dress easier to put on without help, even working-class American women from the 1830s and on would have done their best to keep up with current trends (2015, p. 10). By the 1870s, closely following the latest fashion was within the reach of many, not just the elite.

> "The availability of the sewing machine and the success of American fabric makers were critical factors, and equally important was the development of a system of standardized proportional measurements, which made possible the cheap production of both patterns and readymade clothing. Added to this, vast improvements in transportation and marketing were developed during…(the 1870s) …There was, consequently, by this time no hamlet too insignificant or removed to receive the pattern catalogs and ladies' magazines or to have available a selection of fabrics, pattern systems, and sewing machines, almost as soon as they were available in the Eastern cities…The latest news about making fashionable garments was printed monthly, and patterns were eagerly exchanged." (Severa, 1995, pp. 293 – 295)

One potential source of updated fashion information was Godey's Lady's Book, which was the most popular magazine aimed at women. It boasted 10,000 subscribers in 1839 and 40,000 in 1849. "Personal records indicate that... (ladies' magazines) ...were actually read and studied in the home by every social class and in all areas of the country." (Severa, 1995, p. 3)

Even in light of this information, we can't simply assume that every person in the United States and Indian Territory would have known about or read Godey's Lady's Book. Fortunately for us, there was a direct connection between Godey's Lady's Book and The Cherokee Advocate in 1871.

The Cherokee Advocate newspaper ran, on and off, from 1844 until 1906. The Cherokee National Council authorized the weekly publication, and its aim was to inform the Cherokee people about "their people and the United States" (Pate, 2010). In March of 1871, nestled below a help-wanted ad seeking "twenty good and well-qualified teachers" for the Cherokee Nation's public schools and an exuberant advertisement for a "STEAM FLOURING MILL" that is "Twelve Miles East of Hildebrand's Mill!" in Bloomfield, Arkansas, is the following recommendation:

> "Godey's Lady's Book – This is justly one of the best known and most liked Magazines in the Territory. No lady of any pretensions to refinement should be without it, or some other publication of the same kind of equal merit, though of the latter we honestly confess ourselves unable to specify a single one. But it is not surprising that the Lady's book is so great a favorite. It has the advantages of all the others of its class in age and sterling excellence. Some lady should get up a club at very Post-office. Nothing gives so good an opinion of the intelligence and taste of the fair hostess who bids

her friends welcome, than to be introduced to a neat table covered with readable publications, and especially having Godey's Lady's Book to amuse and instruct one when conversation flags, as it does sometimes and as it ought to, before it turns to gas." (Boudinot, 1871, 5th column on the 4th page)

The editor at Godey's Lady's Book either had a wide correspondence, a voracious appetite for newspaper reading, or used a clipping service, because this didn't escape notice. In May of that year, the *Cherokee Advocate's* mention was paraphrased in a way that was perhaps calculated to pull open the purse strings of the men in the Territory.

"GOOD advice for the Cherokee Nation – Now is the time to get up clubs for the LADY'S BOOK, the oldest, best, and most popular Magazine published in America. There should be one club in the vicinity of every post-office in the country, got up by some lady who only has to ask a few of her male acquaintances to subscribe as a gift to their wives, and it is done, or our Cherokee husbands are not what we take them to be, the worse for them. What a help to conversation and entertainment is the presence of such an attractive publication upon the centre-table of a courteous hostess. What a periodical source of pleasure to the hostess herself, and to her family. As an indication, it tells of intelligence, refinement, and taste; a love of the beautiful, pure, and true, which every man should wish to foster in his 'home circle.' – Advocate, Tahlequah Cherokee Nation." (Hale, 1871a,b, p. 481)

Encouraging readers to get up "clubs" for subscriptions saved the readers money and increased subscription numbers for magazines. In the same year, relative newcomer Harper's Bazaar advertised itself as available for $4 for a year (or six subscriptions for $20) plus $0.20 for shipping (Hearst Corporation, 1871, p. 271).

In 1871, Godey's Lady's Book was less expensive at $3 per year or four for $10 or six for $14 (Hale, 1871a,b, inside cover). To put that cost in context, the salary advertised for the teachers' positions in the *Cherokee Advocate* was an average of $400 per year, and the daily wage for a woman working as a dressmaker in Massachusetts was $1.35 per day (United States Department of Labor, 1929, p. 219). A (male) farm laborer in New York made an average of $1.50 per day (United States Department of Labor, 1929, p. 225). The cost of a Godey's Lady's Book subscription was not a small amount of money, but it wasn't an aspirational luxury.

Neither was it unlikely to be noticed in Indian Territory, where Cherokee public life included a love of literature and the arts.

> "The Cherokee Male and Female Seminaries did more than educate an elite group of Cherokees following eastern standards. Activities at both schools included literary discussions and debates…reading, writing, and dramatic skills and interests continued after the students left school through social societies that emphasized the ongoing study of literature and history. Adults read and discussed literature and made presentations on their readings to their fellows…societies seemed to appeal not only to the upper crust of society but to many others as well." (Parins, 2003, p. 93)

The social perils of ignoring fashion trends can be overstated, but one young lady's tale from an 1871 visit from her village of Germantown to the larger Milwaukee shows that quick thinking sometimes had to fill in the gaps.

> "When I had put on my new black dress, she thought it was very nice and becoming but it needed just one thing – a bustle. Not having one she would make me one. She found a piece of white goods, filling it with newspapers and putting strings to it and I put it on. It seemed all right except that it shortened my dress in the back, which she said it couldn't be helped and wouldn't be noticed with my coat on. I couldn't see why it was necessary to go in style to church, but after getting there I would have felt very much out of place if I hadn't been fixed up." (Severa, 1995, p. 296)

Would Polly have used a sewing machine?

With (potential) fashion inspiration in hand, we come to the nuts and bolts of any sewing endeavor. Namely, would Polly have had access to, and used, a sewing machine? The answer changes over time but may be different depending on which part of the dress is under scrutiny (Fig. 4.1).

Modern industrial clothing production methods have created an abundance of clothing that would have been unimaginable to people in the nineteenth century. It is easy to forget that there was a time when fabric and thread "mills did not have the

Fig. 4.1 Seamstress with sewing machine from 1853. No known restrictions on publication.

capability of producing the vast amounts of fabric to make (sewing) machines viable" (Severa, 1995, p. 293).

> "…the sewing machine was not so much the cause as one of the results of the changes in the clothing industry…sewing machines could have been developed at least twenty years earlier than they were, as a number of people were already working on models in the 1820s… Developments of the sewing machine were made during the fifties and sixties, and by the 1870s all of the variables were in place to make it profitable to install machines in every factory. The many women displaced from their jobs were then employed, at reduced wages, to sew undergarments and shirts and to do the hand-finishing on machine-made garments – a very good deal for the manufacturer." (Severa, 1995, p. 293)

These changes in industrial production allowed sewing machines to reach the home-sewing market.

> "(In the 1870s) …The social importance of the sewing machine is not to be denied, yet its direct role was to provide more people with more and better clothing for less money. Because American women everywhere now had access to good fabrics and had learned to cut and sew, no fashion, however new and elaborate, was denied any of them. Their individual boundaries were limited only by the amount of time available and their degree of skill, given that they could afford fabric." (Severa, 1995, pp. 294–295)

Joan Severa shares an observation on this time period from Joan Jensen and Sue Davidson's *A Needle, A Bobbin, a Strike: Women Needleworkers in America*, "…the sewing machine did not save time. Rather, as with other so-called labor-saving devices for the home, it increased expectations." (1995, p. 295)

When we started the Polly Beck project, we both had strong general experience in modern sewing. Lisa had been working on eighteenth-century-style clothes for about three years but had only made a couple of 1870s petticoats before getting sidetracked away from nineteenth-century ensembles. Lisa initially veered away from the entire nineteenth century because it felt like a field that had been partially co-opted by racists. Reading "Confederates in the Attic" without the benefit of exposure to the work of scholars including Cheyney McKnight and Joseph McGill, Jr. made the entire era seem unfriendly to antiracists. The global pandemic shut down such events anyway, so we couldn't begin with the usual in-person relationships that traditionally drive modern craft and sewing knowledge-sharing.

When we decided to actually interpret Polly Beck's lifetime, we had to start over from the skin out. We had two advantages that allowed us to jump into constructing nineteenth-century clothes without joining the larger community of Dickens Fairs and Civil War Battle reenactors without the chance to get to know people first: the era's own love of instruction manuals and Madame Askew.

This journey may have paralleled Polly's own dress education. The Workwoman's Guide, by "A Lady," is one of the core extant books on the topic of cutting out, sewing up, and even washing clothes from the late 1830s. This book provided us with the instructions to drape bodice linings and draft the sleeves, shifts, and caps essential to dressing in earlier nineteenth-century decades.

We learned the needed construction techniques by combining a little in-person collaboration with the study of paper patterns, written descriptions of complete garments, and fashion plates.

Our ensembles include many custom, reasonably period-accurate pieces. However, to save time and effort, some off-the-rack pieces and pieces by Lara were made with modern sewing techniques, including the use of a serger, a style of machine that wasn't available to home sewists until the 1980s.

When considering whether machine sewing is appropriate, Lara likes to recount a conversation she overheard between Civil War reenactors in 2003. One had a brand-new sewing machine and was exclaiming over its speed and agility. Her friend said, "I wonder what our ancestors would think if they saw something like that." A third reenactor jumped in, "They would say, 'I WANT ONE!'"

Lara also prefers to use modern techniques where they are practical and won't show on the outside of the work.

Working out the details

"Without proper foundations, there can be no fashion"
—Christian Dior (1954) (Lynn, 2014, p. 7).

One problem with relying on extant instruction manuals and advertisements is that the authors assumed the viewers knew how to wear the clothes. You can puzzle out how to cut a shift from books and grasp that you should wear petticoats and corsetry to shape your figure and support the garments, but not when and in what order you would wear all the possible layers to achieve the silhouette of your chosen time and place. Even secondary sources like "The History of Underclothes" by C. Willett and Phillis Cunningham, which helpfully lists underclothing layers from the skin out and mentions that, "we cannot appreciate the significance of the outer form unless we understand the nature of the supporting garments underneath" (p. 13), do not advise the modern person on *how* to wear their nineteenth-century-style underclothes. Whether or not "clothes make the man," it must be said that undergarments make, or break, a dress. A garment from the 1800s simply cannot look the way it should without them.

Madame Askew came to our rescue. Madame Askew is the public persona of our dear friend who dresses in flamboyant, steampunk versions of late nineteenth-century clothes. She was one of the key speakers at the Twins N Needles launch in the spring of 2019, demonstrating the layers worn by a "Victorian Lady" and teaching our students how to build a pillbox-style hat. We grew up with her and knew that her values aligned well with ours. Best of all, we felt comfortable sending her photos of ourselves in our nineteenth-century underthings to help check fit, suggest improvements, and tutor us on the layers needed to achieve specific silhouettes.

Madame Askew confirmed the high quality of Izabela Pitcher's *Victorian Dressmaker* books, vouched for the authenticity of the pattern drafting offered by Truly Victorian patterns, and suggested the best fabrics to construct breathable, comfortable garments.

Lisa's comments on the start of the project

Encouraged by Madame Askew, I started gathering the materials I needed to make a late Victorian-inspired ensemble in 2019, well before we started working on depicting Polly. Originally, I didn't want to start with sewing my undergarments. Like many people, I wanted to get to fitting and constructing an actual dress as soon as possible, so I looked for reliable vendors for the first two layers: the chemise and the corset. I had worn garments by Recollections before, and I was delighted to find that they offer a "combinations" petticoat, which I would now probably call a bodiced petticoat. Redthreaded corsets offered an off-the-shelf mid-nineteenth-century corset that fit my figure reasonably well.

I made up three petticoats and a canvas "Travel" style bustle based on the "Stiff Lace Bustle" in the October 7, 1871 issue of Harper's Bazaar (Fig. 4.2). I began constructing my first 1870s skirt

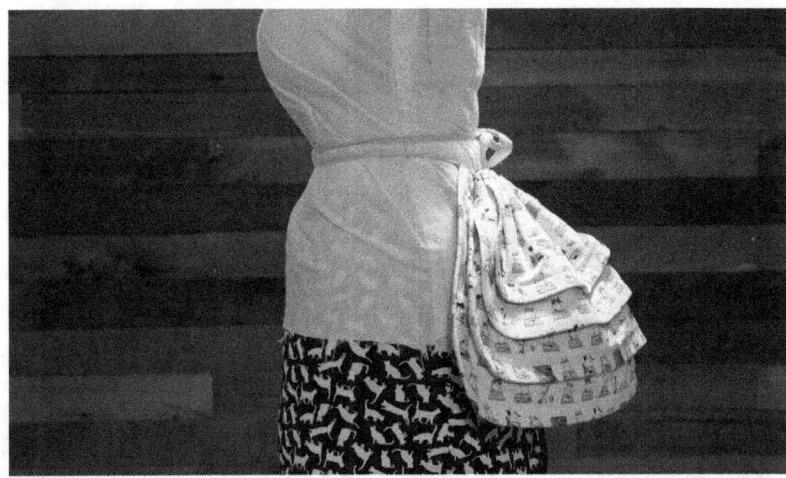

Fig. 4.2 Lisa's first travel bustle. Photo by Lara Neel.

and worked with a local couture designer, Susan Khalje, to fit an adjusted version of the Truly Victorian "Alexandra" bodice. I took some time to find just the right buttons and scheduled the bodice into my mid-2020 sewing plans, wanting to improve my tailoring skills before cutting into my expensive silk. The ensemble was meant to be a celebration of my technical skill, possibly worn to a friend's tea party. I didn't originally plan to use this style as anything more than a flamboyant dress-up opportunity (Fig. 4.2).

So when Lara and I started planning the Polly Beck project as a joint project in late 2021, we did have a head start on the initial garments for the 1870s look, including a corset that fit Lara very well. We pulled the nearly finished silk skirt out of my unfinished projects pile and started seriously considering the options and limitations of Polly's life and time frame.

In the absence of primary, extant garments to examine, we had to map out the boundaries of Polly's choices through other means. For the earlier decades of Polly's adult life during the upheavals leading up to and following the Removal, we ended up supplementing the Workwoman's Guide drafting diagrams with the shapes in "The Victorian Dressmaker: Making Victorian Clothes for Women" by Isabella Pitcher. For construction techniques, we incorporated the advice included in the paper patterns produced by Past Patterns, a sewing pattern company run by Saundra Ros Altman in the United States, and Black Snail Patterns, a sewing pattern company based in Europe. Their focus on copying, then grading extant pieces and offering detailed notes on wearing the styles, gave us a virtual window into early nineteenth-century styles otherwise not available to us for direct study. While the products made by these companies are primarily marketed as sewing patterns, we used them as alternatives to hands-on study of the garments referenced by their instructions and starting points for further research on silhouettes.

Searching for information on garments actually worn in Indian Territory or simply west of the Mississippi River, we found the publications of Marna Jean Davis and Elizabeth Stewart Clark.

Marna Jean Davis' self-published book, "No Lady of Leisure: Clothing for the Victorian and Edwardian Working Woman," draws on women's personal diaries, advertisements, newspaper articles, photographs, sketches, and extant garments to describe the cut, construction, and styling of clothes of the majority of women wearing European-American dress in the nineteenth century. Her work focuses on the 1860s forward but includes some examples from as early as the 1830s. This was especially helpful for us because her time frame overlapped considerably with ours. Further, she presents the material through the eyes of the experienced dressmaker she is, describing not only silhouettes but construction methods, specific stitch choices, seam line placements, and ease guidelines. She provides two pages on apron styles as part of her attempt to rectify that the, "often-neglected part of fashion history is the "everyday" clothing that women wore during their daily routines (Davis, 2015, p. 62)."

Moving from description to creation, Elizabeth Stewart Clark's "The Dressmaker's Guide" provided us with drafting, pattern adjustment, and construction methods specific to the 1840s to the 1860s.

Choosing years to depict

When we started talking about the Polly Beck project, we originally planned to make up two sets of garments aiming for the decade that Polly was about our age at the time. She would have been in her early 40s in the mid-1860s. We knew this decade would have complexities. We expected to address or integrate acknowledgment that we didn't share the values of many modern Americans who intensively interact with that era.

We knew Cherokee people were not safe from the ravages of the Civil War (Confer, 2007) and assumed Polly faced difficulties alongside her countrymen and women.

However, when we got together in early 2023 to drape bodice patterns and dig through Lisa's fabric storage, we found ourselves hesitating to commit to depicting such a cataclysm. Having recently endured the international disruption of the COVID-19 pandemic, we didn't want to dwell on a time when our family suffered a second major catastrophe in the same generation.

What goes into these ensembles

This may sound a bit shocking, but Lara and Lisa both find drawers[4] deeply uncomfortable. They wear modern underpants (or nothing) under their chemises, with no one the wiser. Feel free to tell their secret. Elizabeth Stewart Clark, in *The Dressmaker's Guide: 1840–1865*, seems to support their decision when she writes,

> "While chemises and corsets are essentially universal, drawers are a more optional garment for mid-century. They can be accurately worn all through the era, though they may be a bit over-represented in living history as opposed to actual history when we're looking specifically at the earliest years of the era…with any pattern, expect to do some adjustment to the depth of the crotch and the width of the drawers. Too little depth, or too little width, and you will not be comfortable (vast potential for Gapping and Extreme Wedgies)" (2009, p. 141) (Fig. 4.3).

We must take a moment to nod to nomenclature. According to Elizabeth Stewart Clark,

> "In modern living history, we often use the term 'corset' to describe a steel-boned, fashion-shaping undergarment, and the term 'stays' to describe a more gently-fitted undergarment with shaping provided from few bones, or cording and quilting…in original sources…(the two) terms are used fairly interchangeably" (2009, p. 117).

Even the gorgeous book, "Stays, or a Corset: Shaping Underclothing and Undergarments from the Second Half of the 18th Century Until the First Half of the 20th Century" by Veronika Sulcova and Dana Szemalyova, does not provide a clear line

How we "dressed" Polly to bring her into the picture   119

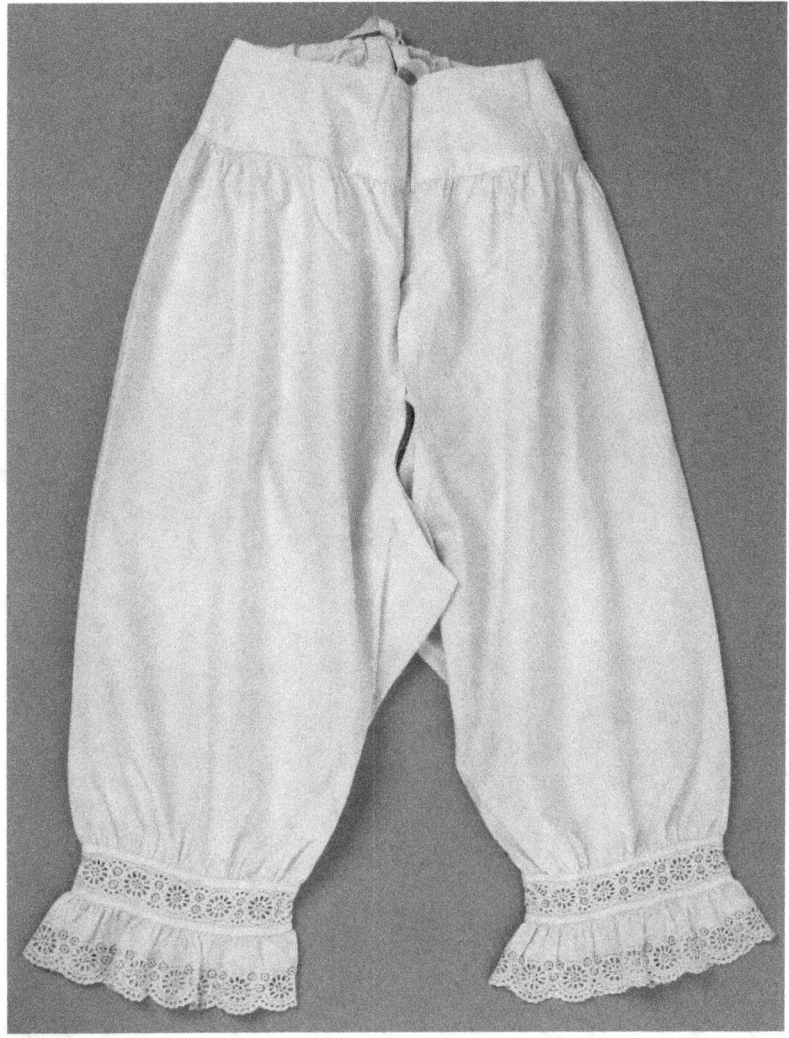

Fig. 4.3 Drawers from the 1840s. Public domain.

distinguishing the garments as distinct styles. We will follow the modern convention of dividing the two terms or simply calling the garment what the person who either made it or designed the pattern called it. However, when a particular style of support garment isn't specified, we will use the term "corset" just to reduce confusion (Figs. 4.4 and 4.5).

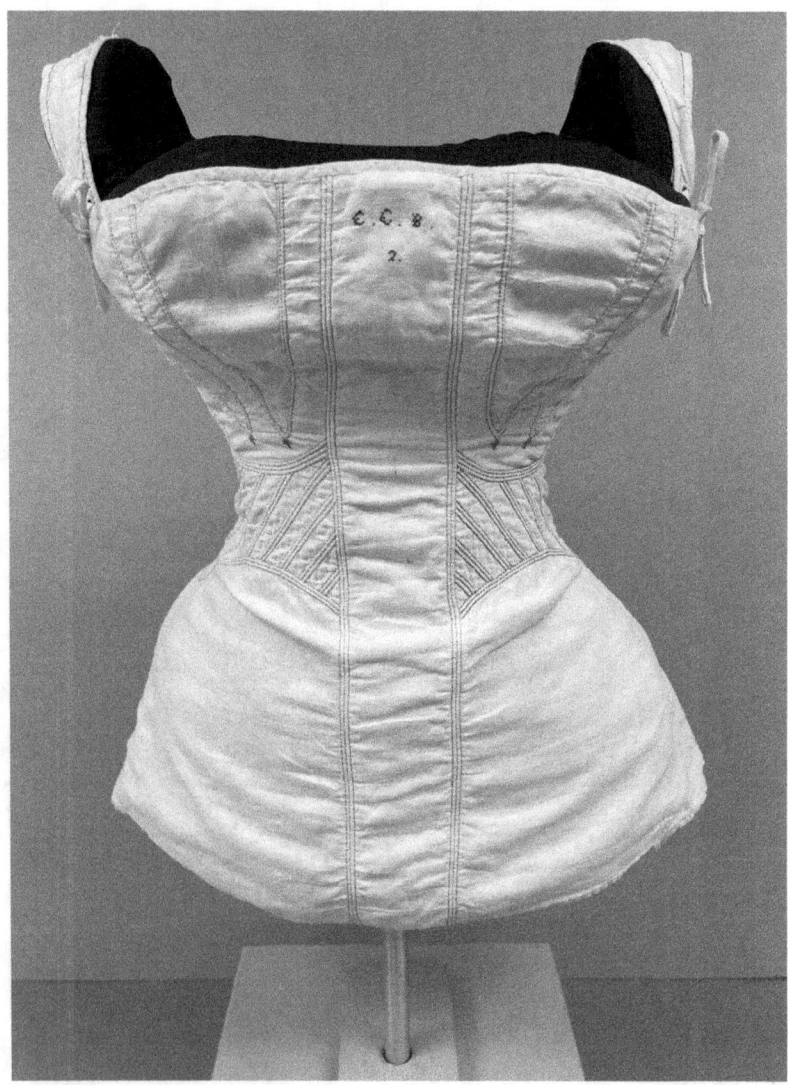

Fig. 4.4 Soft corset with contrasting blue thread pattern from 1820 to 1830. Bruce & Susan Greene Costume Collection patterned by Genesee Country Village & Museum curator Brandon Brooks. Image used with kind permission.

Advances in technology and materials allowed corsets to evolve throughout their history (Brooks, 2024), starting with the move

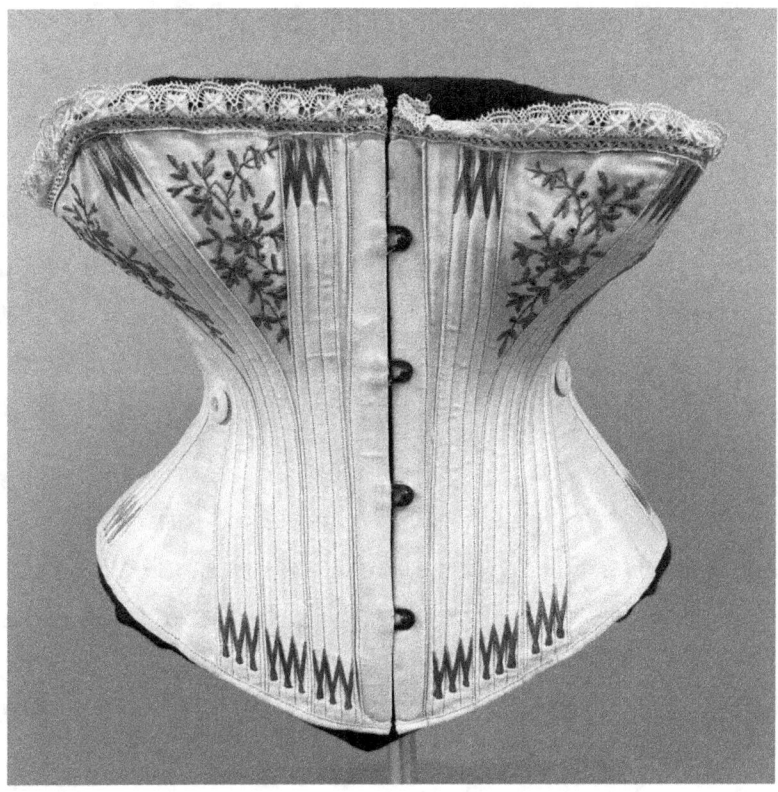

Fig. 4.5 Ivory sateen corset made between 1869 and 1872. Bruce & Susan Greene Costume Collection patterned by Genesee Country Village & Museum curator Brandon Brooks. Image used with kind permission.

from whalebone[5] to steel bones at the beginning of the 1900s to "lighter girdles in the 1920s and 1930s." According to Eleri Lynn in *Underwear: Fashion in Detail*, some form of corsetry was worn by most women until the 1960s. "It was only then that foundationwear was replaced by diet and exercise as a method of figure control – along with a little help from tensile new fabrics such as Lycra." (2014, p. 73)

Corsets are possibly the most asked-about and controversial part of any historic ensemble. It could be that some of the myths and fears around corsets are echoes of messaging from dress reformers, working together with images of fainting ladies in historical fiction. Known as artistic, hygienic, or rational dress, depending on the time period, dress reformers were a minority movement active from around 1850 (when Amelia Bloomer invented what came to be called the Bloomer costume in New York) until World War I (Newton, 1974, pp. 1–3). Exact complaints varied, but most dress reformers decried the wearing of tight corsets and heavy petticoats (Lynn, 2014, p. 222) (Fig. 4.6).

In *Fashioning the Bourgeoisie,* Philippe Perrot argues that shaping the body with an undergarment "was viewed mainly as a continuation of (an infant's) swaddling clothes, as a protective mold" that began as early as Roman times and continued through the 1700s, but that corsets and other support garments, starting with the "Ninon" corset around 1810, actually do something else. "This new armor…corresponded to an image of the female body as a softness to be supported and a waist to be compressed. The intent was hygienic and aesthetic: to strengthen a basically weak anatomy and enhance its privileged aspects." According to him, vocal detractors of corseting predate even this change, starting around 1750, with a "medical-pedagogical crusade" that was taken up by several public figures and medical experts, Jean-Jacques Rousseau among them. The primary effect of this endeavor wasn't the banishing of corsets, but rather the championing of a combination of physical education and "orthopedic" corsets thought to promote better health (1994, pp. 150–151).

Split busks, first patented by French corsetier Jean-Julien Josselin in 1829, certainly make wearing a corset easier, as lacing must only be loosened, not removed, to open or close the front of the

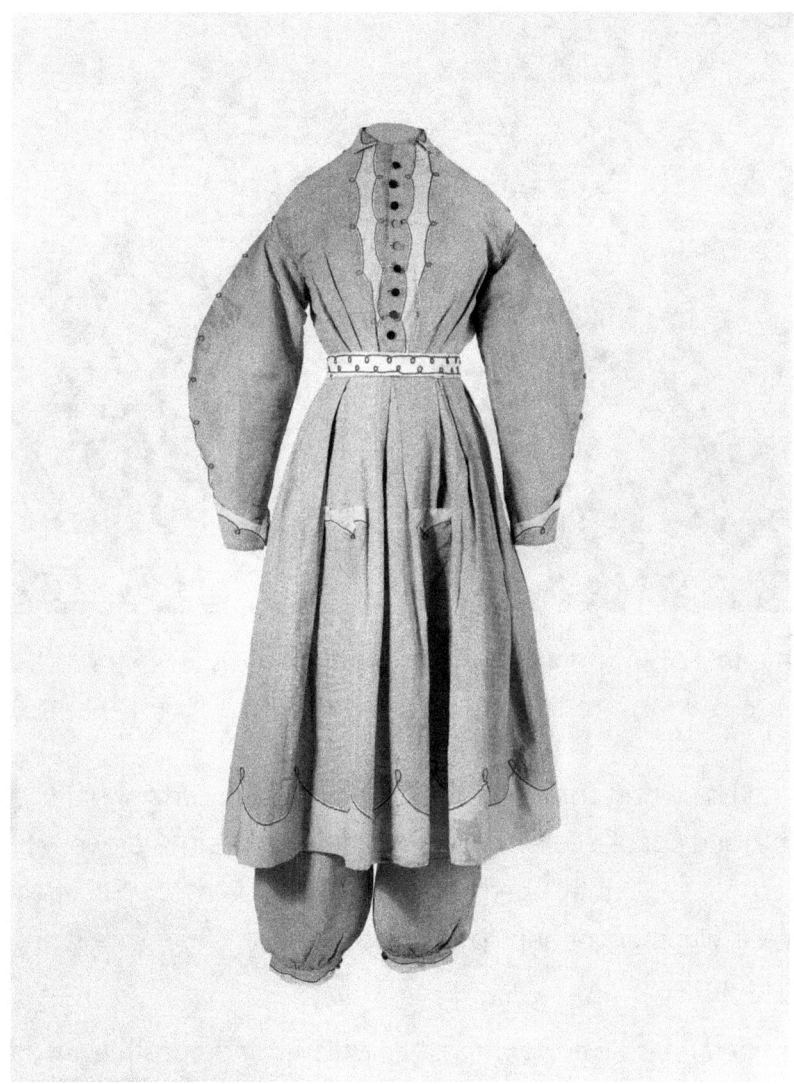

Fig. 4.6 Styles similar to this "gymnasium" suit were better known as Bloomer costumes. Public domain.

corset and slip it on or off (Lynn, 2014, p. 86). This, along with slot-and-stud front fastenings, allowed for the development of lacing 'a la paresseuse,' or lazy lacing[6], in 1843 (Lynn, 2014, p. 119). Lara

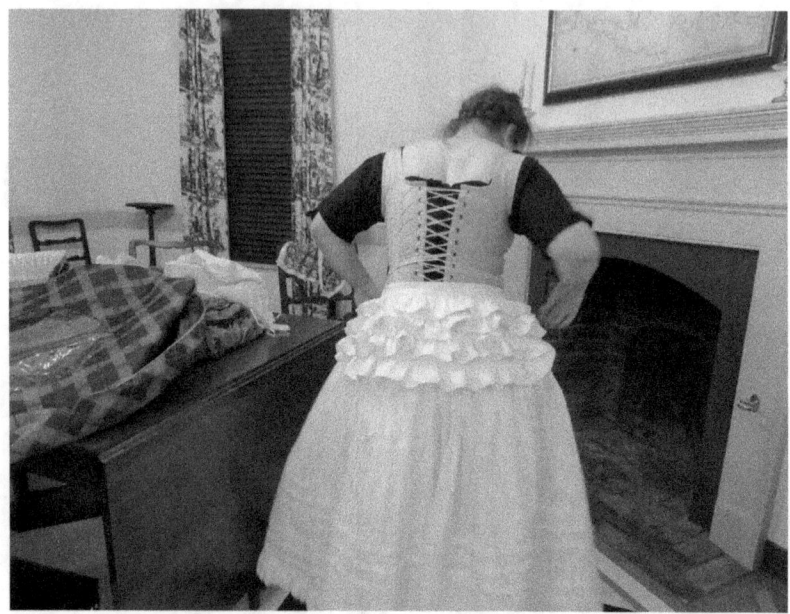

Fig. 4.7 Lisa in her 1830s style stays laced a la paresseuse. She has a black chemise, three petticoats, and a ruffled bustle on as well. Photo by Lara Neel.

and Lisa report that, with a little practice, one certainly can get into and out of a corset with very little, or no, help. A properly fitted, not-too-tightly-laced corset should not be uncomfortable to wear, whether or not help is needed to finish closing the lacing[7] (Fig. 4.7).

A chemise is always worn as the first layer, underneath even the corset. This protects the wearer's skin from any rubbing against the corset and also protects the corset from skin oils and perspiration. Similarly to the corset, a chemise may also be called by its earlier name, a shift. "Chemise" as a term came into fashion in the late 1700s from the French (Cumming et al., 2010, p. 46 and p. 184). Lara and Lisa call each undergarment what the pattern-maker or garment-maker calls the garment (Fig. 4.8).

How we "dressed" Polly to bring her into the picture   125

Fig. 4.8 Chemise from the 1830s. Public domain.

Another layer of clothing lies between the corset and the outer dress. As with the two other garments we have seen, it had more than one name that evolved over time.

> "This new garment appeared early in the 1840's, and was frequently spoken of as a 'waistcoat.' Made of white longcloth and shaped to the waist by goring, it covered the corset, and thus took the place of the flap front of the old type of chemise, which used to hang down over the top of the corset to conceal it from accidental view" (Willett and Cunnington, 1992, p. 147).

From the 1860s through the 1880s, it was called a "petticoat bodice" (Willett and Cunnington, 1992, p. 180). In modern circles, it is usually called a corset cover but is also known as a camisole (Fig. 4.9).

All other items that sit underneath the visible skirt of the dress come under the general heading of "skirt supports." The proper skirt supports help bring a dress to life, with the corset being the only undergarment more important to the overall silhouette.

Skirt supports, meant primarily to hold up the back of the dress, have undergone many changes of style, have gone in and out of fashion, and have a cornucopia of names, from a "foxes' tail" in 1343 to a "dress improver" or "tournure" in 1889. Steel half-hoop bustles known as "crinolettes" were popular from 1865 to 1876 (Cumming et al., 2010, p. 35). Even within the same general time period, the exact style, size, and audacity of the bustle vary

Fig. 4.9 Corset Cover from 1870. Public domain.

according to the exact year represented, the wearer's taste, the occasion at hand, and the materials available (Fig. 4.10).

Petticoats provide lift to the outer skirts while smoothing over any lumps or bumps caused by the bustle. The 1840s are famous as a time when petticoats were especially numerous (Cumming et al., 2010, p. 155). Perrot reports that "as many as a dozen"

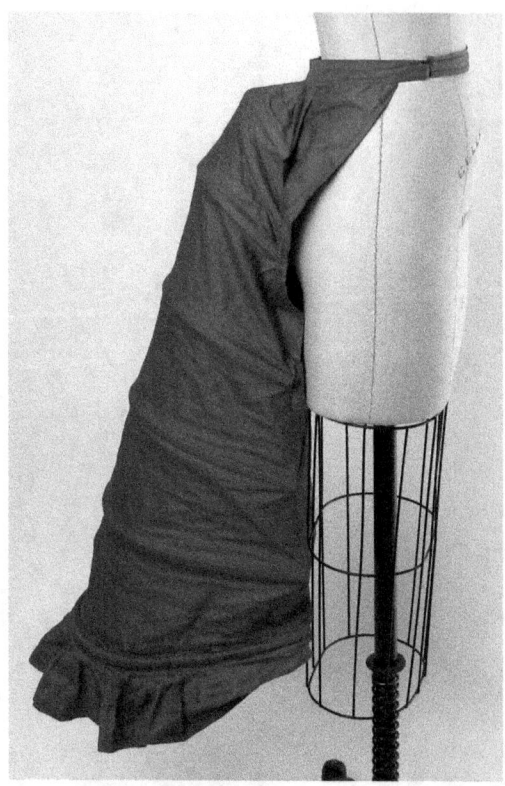

Fig. 4.10 This red cotton bustle from the 1870s shows a flair for color. Public domain.

petticoats would have been needed for some silhouettes. This changed around the mid-1850s, with the invention of the cage crinoline, which may have only needed one or two petticoats over it (1994, p. 159). The volume created by the bustle in the 1870s also allowed fewer petticoats to be worn (Fig. 4.11). Even Amelia Bloomer gave up her controversial style of dress for the crinoline, partly because it was more comfortable than the heavy petticoats in vogue earlier in the 1850s (Newton, 1974, p. 3).

Fig. 4.11 The tucks in the lower half of this 1855–1865 petticoat help give it more body. Public domain.

Accessories, which include everything else, from bonnets to necklaces to shoes to chemisettes and even sleeves, are ignored at the living historian's peril. People in the past, as now, built their wardrobes over time, so it can be difficult to feel that an ensemble is truly finished. There's always a new-to-you parasol, fan, or cap to catch the eye and encourage one to reach for their purse or run to the sewing table (Fig. 4.12).

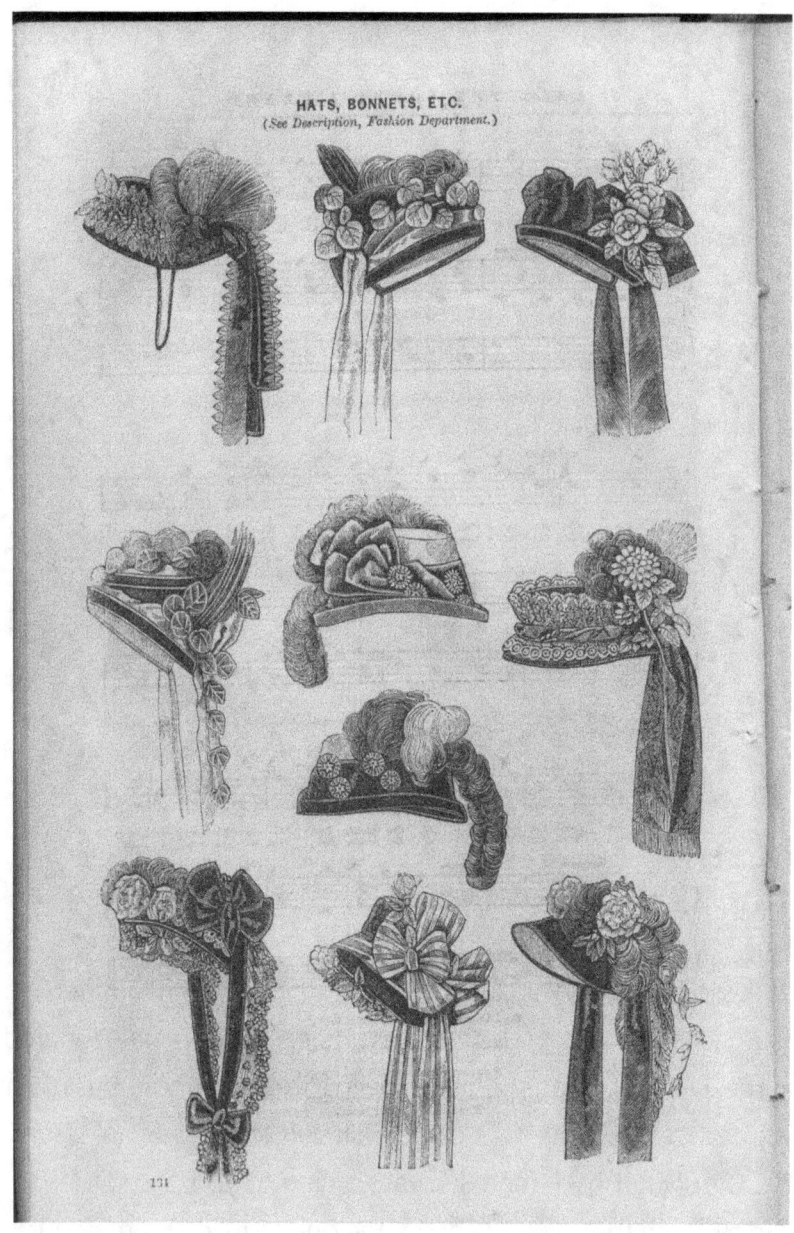

Fig. 4.12 This profusion of hat styles from the February 1871 edition of Godey's Lady's Book shows a variety of shapes but also shows how intensely decorated hats were in this time period.

Lisa's comments on her 1838 Biedermeier "Calico"

Our first completed Polly ensemble began almost as a joke (Fig. 4.13).

Lisa: "Hey, if we want to make people uncomfortable, we can lean into the controversy around the Treaty of New Echota and make a late 1830's depiction."

Lara: "Can you do that?"

Lisa: "Well, I had those 1830's stays made in 2021, but I haven't made anything to go over them."

Lara: "So you can. What if?"

Lisa: "Yeah, what if…"

Later, Lara pulled some printed cotton from Lisa's fabric pile. "Is this SATEEN?"

Lisa: "The card says I have…10 yards of it. It's a reproduction Biedermeier print by Sartor. They said it's an 1820's – 1840's design."

Lara probably knew better than to ask why I bought ten yards of fabric and paid to ship it from Europe without having a specific project in mind. It's a gorgeous, medium red with brilliant blue flowers and yellow and green details.

Being reminded of this perfect fabric cemented this project for me. I fetched the 1830s stays to take my measurements in them and started flipping through my copy of *Patterns of Fashion 1: the content, cut, construction and context of Englishwomen's dress c.1720–1860.*

Fig. 4.13 Lisa in her 1838 Biedermeier "Calico." Photo by Lara Neel.

We started researching the silhouette of the late 1830s looking toward the 1840s:

"The latest cut and silhouette, extrapolated from the exaggerated fashion plates, were followed by all as faithfully as bodily limitations allowed; but the illustrated, elaborate surface decorations and accessories were adopted more conservatively." (Severa, 1995, p. 4)

> "Styles for women in the 1840s reflected not only a wearer's modesty but also a popular trend toward extreme bodily constriction and the inhibition of natural movement. In the very beginning of the decade, fashion illustrations began showing a rigid, bust-altering bodice shape and floor-length skirts with voluminous petticoats, which tended toward one basic silhouette: a rounded triangle that sloped down from the neck and shoulders and a severely constricted long torso with a flattened, upward-spreading bust and a full, bell-shaped skirt brushing the ground. Even given the observable variations in waist length and sleeve style, a woman's silhouette was quite similar throughout the decade, whether in working or better dress." (Severa, 1995, p. 7) (Fig. 4.14)]

All of this meant that I needed to start over on my petticoats to get that soft bell shape. I also needed a new shift, since I didn't like how my 1870s shift felt under my corded stays.

For about 12 weeks, I sewed petticoat after petticoat and tested a number of shift styles before designing a shift, then fitting and constructing the gown.

Ultimately, this ensemble requires the following pieces and accessories:

Fig. 4.14 This dress is a typical 1838 shape. Public domain.

Shift

Based on a short aside from "The Workwoman's Guide," I drafted a gored shift with straps that had little flaps to button onto my stays. This button-on extension to the neckline allows the shift to remain out of sight along the wide necklines of the decade while accommodating the very dramatic shape of the stays. In the 19th century, shifts (also known as chemises) were made of "linen, homespun, or cotton" (Cumming et al., 2010, p. 46). I chose linen because I find it more comfortable and easier to care for than cotton. In Fig. 4.7, you can see the back of the prototype shift covering my back and arms.

Under-petticoat

I drafted and made a muslin for some open drawers, which modern nineteenth-century enthusiasts appear to wear almost universally based on blog posts and YouTube videos. I didn't like how they felt on my body and decided to wear a linen under-petticoat instead. It's the simplest possible skirt: a hemmed tube gathered into a waistband.

Corded petticoat with lining

Based on a study of extant petticoats published in Jennifer Rosbrugh's book, "The Corded Petticoat Sewing Workbook," I made up a corded petticoat from cotton organdy with a long, boned waistband adjusted from Black Snail pattern number 0321. This was the first layer that really started the bell-like silhouette visible in fashion plates and descriptions of the era.

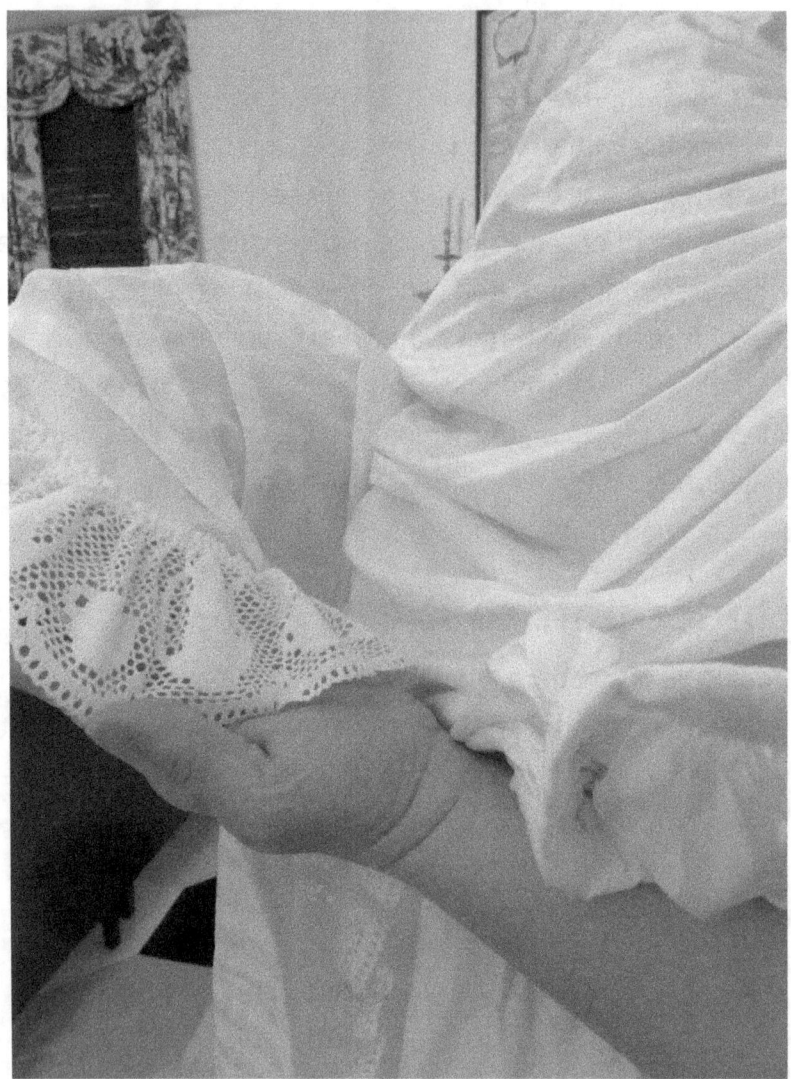

Fig. 4.15 Tucked petticoat detail. Photo by Lara Neel.

Tucked sateen petticoat with lace flounce

I planned this petticoat out using descriptions from Elizabeth Stewart Clark's publications. It's too far to call it "patterned" since it's just a straight tube, straight tucks, and a simple waistband. It was great practice for cartridge pleats! (Fig. 4.15).

1830s corded stays

I ordered my custom stays from Redthreaded in 2021 as a commission. While they were adjusted to my proportions, they're based on a pair held by the Daughters of the American Revolution museum in Washington, D.C. The pair is accession number 48.49.1.

> The original was "Said to have been worn by Margaret Johnson Seeber, wife of Abraham Seeber. Margaret was born in New York, her parents having moved there from Connecticut. She was born in 1812 and probably married about 1834-35, as her daughter Mary Elizabeth was born in 1836. The family is in Caroga, Fulton County, NY in the 1850 census. Based on the style of the corset and its decoration, and the fact that it was saved in such good condition, it seems possible that this was her wedding corset. The donor was Margaret's granddaughter" (Daughters of the American Revolution, collections.dar.org).

These stays have a beautiful, fanciful pattern of cording, which provides some soft shaping. The only rigidity to them comes from the wide, wooden busk straight down the front. Because they predate separating busks of later in the nineteenth century, they lace up the back. I can get into them by myself, but it's faster with help. The back is visible in Fig. 4.7, and the front detail is shown here in Fig. 4.16.

Fig. 4.16 Stays front detail, including both main and lining fabric of 1830s dress. Photo by Lisa Neel.

There is some debate in the historic clothing community about wearing petticoats over stays or under them. Since candid photography of people in their underwear wasn't possible until well after the 1840s, people trying to decide their order of dress have to guess based on the silhouette of the outer garments as captured in portraits and cartoons from magazines like Punch, which are often lampooning or sexualizing the fashion being depicted.

I chose to wear my petticoats under the stays for this ensemble, since I am very short waisted,[8] and the ideal silhouette of this decade includes a pointed center front bodice. Wearing the stays on top of my petticoats allows the stays busk to help press down on the petticoats at the center front. This avoids the gown's front point, which is very lightly supported by narrow pieces of artificial whalebone sewn snugly into the seam allowance, fighting for its life against 3–5 layers of gathered, shirred, and pleated cotton.

Small bustle

I bought a ruffled hip pad from Gibson Girl Dress, a specialist dress shop in Ukraine. I could have easily made this piece, but I wanted to support this budding company, and, honestly, I was burned out on sewing white ruffles by then! This piece buttons to my stays as well, over my petticoats. It gives the back of my gown a little extra shape to the back rather than a dramatic bustle. This is visible in Fig. 4.7.

Chemisette

I bought a chemisette designed and made by Laura Barbatano, a dressmaker selling her work on the Etsy platform from Italy. This fills in the neckline of the gown for day wear, protecting my skin from the sun and lending the gown a delicate, easily washed collar.

> "Chemisette" from about 1800 to the 1850s, meant a sleeveless white muslin or cambric garment that was used similarly to a modern dickey. After 1860, it *can* mean a long-sleeved blouse, depending on the context, but it can also be the same as the earlier use" (Cumming et al., 2010, p. 46).

Gown

> "To achieve a perfect fit in the bodice and sleeves of this period, one had to be or hire a good seamstress...The practice was to measure each customer carefully and to cut the bodice so that it was smoothly fitted, with no ease whatsoever, over the corseted body" (Severa, 1995, p. 8).

I combined design elements from *Patterns of Fashion 1: the content, cut, construction and context of Englishwomen's dress c.1720–1860* number 44 "c. 1837–1841 Morning Dress in brown silk with bishop sleeves" with Black Snail pattern number 0221 and built the bodice on a lining that Lara draped onto me using the directions from The Workwoman's Guide. I used the notes from Past Patterns number 806 to make specific length and width choices for the skirt.

Made from the red, printed cotton sateen, I fully lined it in a second layer of quilting-weight cotton. I chose a printed cotton carried by Burnley and Trowbridge, their Purple Ground "Spot'd & Flower'd" Cotton. This bright, cheerful fabric was based on a late eighteenth-century print. By lining my gown in it, I evoked the possibility that I had taken apart an earlier dress to reuse the fabric.

I added seven loops of corded trim to the upper sleeves, releasing into a dramatic silhouette to the wrist. The loops give some visual interest to the sleeves while referencing the graceful script of the Cherokee written language.

Based on the work of Elizabeth Stewart Clark (2010), I created lightly padded chest shields that extend from the shoulder line to just below the top of my stays. These are often misunderstood in extants as "bust improvers," but they actually prevent the long shoulder line from buckling and do not add to the bustline diameter at all. The period-appropriate nature of this choice is further bolstered by Joan Severa when she writes, "A typical bodice treatment included padding, usually of lambswool, placed above the breast on either side, to lend a soft, triangular shape to the torso that was carried up over the shoulder to some extent" (1995, p. 9).

The faced hem and dust ruffle bring the total yardage in the gown to about 24 yards of fabric. The final edge of the hem is protected from wear by a layer of wool ribbon binding the edge. The hem is "152 inches" around and supported by the layers of petticoats.

> "…women's skirts were made to touch the floor, and a 'hem-saver,' usually a stiff braid of wool and/or horsehair which protected the floor-length skirts from wear, was

> sewn at the hem after 1841. Skirts were lined either fully or merely in the lower portion, where a crisp facing from eight to eighteen inches wide was used as flatlining. The upper edge of this facing was handpicked to the skirt fabric, a technique that meant taking very small vertical stitches (only a thread or two in depth, not too closely together) across the top of the facing, which was usually on a selvage" (Spelling "selvage" is in the original. – Lara) (Severa, 1995, p. 8).

All this is worn with stockings, flat shoes, a linen or cotton cap, and a bonnet (when outdoors).

> "The bonnet was the proper head covering for a lady and hence was worn by women of all classes. Bonnet prices found in personal records ranged from about $3 to $8, though women could buy foundations and trim their own at lesser cost. Most bonnets were low and horizontal in the crown line, with a face-concealing, deep brim that had long, drooping ends reaching below the chin line and a neck curtain, or 'bavolet,' gathered to the back. In the early part of the decade, the brim was quite deep and close to the sides of the face; toward the fifties it opened out into a more circular, somewhat shallower, shape, at the same time retreating toward the back of the head" (Severa, 1995, pp. 10–11).

In all, we calculated that the ensemble cost roughly $2,300 to assemble in 2023. The gown alone took about $498 and 60 hours to construct using a mix of hand and machine sewing.

Hollywood has led us to believe that wearing all this fabric, and especially the stays, would make movement impossible, breathing difficult, and life agony. Even some dress historians describe the slope-shouldered silhouette of this bodice as "restrictive." Lisa has worn this ensemble many times. The width of the skirts makes modern activities such as loading a dishwasher and driving a car awkward, and her cats are a menace when she's getting into the stays, but the customized stays fit comfortably and support the weight of the petticoats and gown around her waist. Once everything's on, the gown is about as unwieldy as a modern ballgown worn with a large petticoat.

Lisa's comments on her 1845 work dress

The simpler silhouette of my 1845 work dress requires only a shift, one or two starched petticoats, the small ruffle bustle from the 1830s ensemble, 1830s stays, flat shoes, and stockings (Fig. 4.17). The outer bodice closes with drawstrings for an adjustable fit and is constructed as a washing dress, a style that Marna Jean Davis explains is, "easily laundered" (p. 35).

This dress was meant to depict Polly during the era of rebuilding in Indian Territory and serve as a conjectured ancestor to the modern Tear Dress. It's heavily influenced by the work of Marna Jean Davis. I wear this with the 1830s stays, so it's still no fun to drive a car with it on because the rigid straps on the stays make turning my body to make a proper shoulder check difficult, but the more modest width and sleeves designed to readily roll up to my elbows make this a comfortable dress to wear, even while scrubbing floors or teaching children how to spin wool into yarn.

Fig. 4.17 Lisa in her 1840s work dress at the Congressional Cemetery. Photo by Steve Andreadis.

Black Snail number 0121 presents the maker with a dress pattern from a specific extant, described as,

> "from the 1840s, made from a fine block printed muslin. This kind of dress would have been worn in the morning, on hot summer days, or as a maternity dress, and is called a wrapper. Made from printed calico fabric this style was worn by women of the working class during the pre-civil war era."

I chose this gown as the core resource to create a mid-1840s work dress, specifically as a historically grounded Tear Dress. Based on my notes from Tonia Hogner Weavel's keynote on Cherokee Tear Dresses from 2019 (Hogner-Weavel) and a 2018 article from Anadisgoi (Dittman, 2018), I added a shoulder yoke, underarm gussets, a bias-cut hem ruffle, and some length and fullness to the sleeve of the outer layer of the dress as visual nods to the standards of the modern Tear Dress that I could document as in use in that decade. While more common in undergarments, Marna Jean Davis has published a description of at least one work dress from the 1860s with underarm and sleeve gussets (p. 20). While these were probably added to this example for wearing ease or repair, underarm gussets are a core element of the modern Tear Dress. I found many examples of full bishop sleeves and yokes in work dresses in the early nineteenth century. Hem ruffles or flounces can be found in many examples of the decade. I was especially taken by object number 1998-232 held at the Art Museum at Colonial Williamsburg (The Colonial Williamsburg Foundation, 2024).

I based the lining on my draped bodice shapes and generally followed the construction order given by Black Snail.

I hand sewed this dress, except for the finishes on some of the trim. This dress took about 8 yards of 45" printed cotton in a meandering green-on-green print. The fabric is modern quilting-weight cotton, and the print is based on a generic nineteenth century calico style, rather than a specific example.

The lining has its own story, not just for the construction but also for the two yards of hand-woven heavy linen. I bought this linen from Sartor in early 2022, when they were selling it as "heirloom linen" (Sartour. *Handwoven vintage linen fabric*). It arrived as promised, unwashed from possibly decades in storage, smelling like it had been kept in a potato cellar. My husband nicknamed it "grave goods linen," and my cats, usually eager to get hair all over my new fabrics, gave it a wide berth. I sincerely wanted to use this special fabric for gown linings without smelling like a terrarium, so I washed it four times, but it stubbornly held onto its dark memories and remained mushroom-colored. I tried every gentle modern detergent in my laundry room with no success. I doused swatches in vodka and sprayed them with hydrogen peroxide. These old standbys didn't remove the faint, organic odor, although the hydrogen peroxide brightened the color.

I was finally able to get the scent out by laying the linen out to dry on a bright, hot summer day after a vigorous hand scrubbing in steaming hot water with Marius Fabre's laundry soap. My hands were pink from the heat transferring through my gloves, but the linen was finally unscented and a uniform, bisque color.

I think all that work was worth it. This fabric was a dream to hand sew, shaped readily under pressing, and accepted hand-sewn eyelets without fraying or requiring me to use pliers.

In contrast to the dramatic "calico" dress, this dress cost about $200 to complete. If I had to buy the other layers down to my shoes and stays, it would have cost about $1,400 to produce in 2021.

Lara's comments on her early 1870s ensemble

I have taken Polly's early 1870s plaid cotton bustle dress through two rounds of improvements (Fig. 4.18). As I believe she would have, my goal is to make my ensemble as fashionable, practical, and comfortable as possible. Although I do wear dresses and skirts frequently, the style and silhouette of a bustle dress is a radical departure from my everyday clothing. Some of the underpinnings would have been familiar to Polly, but some, like the hastily constructed bustle mentioned by the young lady as she was "fixed up" to go to church in Milwaukee, probably would have been new to her as well. From a certain perspective, the bustle, and all of the changes to the skirt and bodice that went with it, marked a sea change in fashion. "Never before had there been so rapid and dramatic a transformation in a woman's silhouette…" (Severa, 1995, p. 301).

On the other hand, dress historian Agnes Young sorted dress styles from 1760 to 1937 into three sets of "contours." With her sorting, it's easier to see how the 1870s bustle style harkens back to similar shapes from the 1780s and 1790s (Perrot, 1994, pp. 22–23) (Fig. 4.19).

It's possible that the bustle fashion's sartorial debt to the 1780s burst from subconscious to conscious in the semi-mania for all things Dolly Varden, which included a polonaise-style dress

Fig. 4.18 Lara in her early 1870s ensemble. Photo by Delonna Milroy.

Fig. 4.19 This dress from 1778 to 1780 shows a "bustled" silhouette. Public domain.

Fig. 4.20 The "Dolly Varden" outfit was certainly eye-catching. No known restrictions on publication.

(Cunnington and Cunnington, 1959, p. 493). This style was popular in Britain and the United States from 1865 to 1875, although it's not clear if this particularly flamboyant look was used as an everyday dress or was confined to costume parties (McCort, 2019) [Fig. 4.20].

Before 2020, I was considering depicting a different time in Polly's life. The COVID-19 pandemic and the Civil War didn't have huge parallels, but in 2023, I craved a project that could speak to renewal and hope rather than survival. I like to think that Polly would have created an ensemble like mine as part of her desire to celebrate putting the past behind her, as well as the birth of her first grandchild. John Beck was born August 17, 1871 (Beck). Spare a thought for his mother, Julia Ann, who at the age of 20 lost her husband[9] when he was killed at the trial of the man who killed her a few months earlier (H.R. Exec. No. 287, 42nd Cong., 2nd Sess. (1872), p. 6).

Corset

I chose an 1860s corset made by Redthreaded. As often happens at the beginning of a decade, fashion styles later associated with the entire decade weren't in evidence for the first few years. I would expect that a woman in 1872 would still wear the "very short-waisted, full-busted corset style...not much changed from the late 1860s type" (Severa, 1995, p. 309). In *Dressed for the Photographer*, Joan Severa points out that "older" people in photographs tend to wear somewhat more out-of-fashion clothes, a phenomenon she calls "fashion lag" (1995, p. xvii). So, even if Polly would have wanted an absolutely up-to-date dress, she may have chosen a corset shape that may have looked slightly old-fashioned to a younger woman at the time.

Chemise

Lisa handed down the petticoat combinations she bought from Recollections to me. I loved the sturdy fabric, and the fit was, overall, very good. The bust of the combinations fit me fairly well when I was not wearing a corset, but it couldn't quite close above the mid-bust once my corset was lifting my bust into the correct (rather high) position. It fit where it mattered, and I simply tucked the unbuttoned top of the garment back toward my shoulders.

In 2024, I made a new chemise for myself using a Truly Victorian pattern and white cotton shirting fabric from my local fabric store. This fabric was a bit thinner than was used for the combinations. I found that having a thinner layer under the corset made it slightly easier to lace up.

Corset Cover

My corset cover is based on a Laughing Moon corset cover pattern that Lisa adjusted to fit my corseted shape more closely. I made it in an easy-to-sew cotton poplin.

Bustle

My first bustle was the canvas "Travel" style bustle made by Lisa using a pattern published by Deb Salisbury, owner of The Mantua-Maker Historical Sewing Patterns. I made a second bustle from a Truly Victorian pattern and boning kit. This combination bustle and petticoat is extremely comfortable and light to wear. It really is easy to sit down in it without having to wrestle it into submission, which is not true of all bustles. I also don't need to wear any other petticoats with this bustle.

Bodice and Outer Skirts

Plaid fabrics din't show up very much in Godey's Lady's Book fashion illustrations at the time, perhaps because they were challenging to print attractively at scale, but that doesn't mean that the mode wasn't worn. *Victorian Fashion in America*, edited by Kristina Harris, includes several striking examples of women's dresses in plaids and checks from the 1860s through the early 1900s (2002, p. 3, 8, 11, 35, 55, 246). An 18-year-old Californian named Alice Warner also wore a bold plaid dress to have her portrait taken in 1870 (Severa, 1995, p. 325) (Fig. 4.21).

Lisa chose a lovely green plaid homespun fabric and gifted it to me to make my bodice and outer skirt. Ten yards may sound like a lot of fabric, but the combination of extra fabric needed to

Fig. 4.21 This unidentified woman wore a plaid dress for her portrait taken by Mathew Brady sometime between 1844 and 1860. No known restrictions on publication.

match the pattern across seams and the relatively narrow width of the fabric led to me using nearly every scrap.

I used the basque, square-neckline version of Marna Jean Davis's Early Bustle Era Basic Bodice Pattern as the basis for my bodice, and, as with most everything, Lisa helped me adjust the side seams and front darts to best suit my corseted figure. Following the patternmaker's advice, I underlined the bodice with cotton sateen. I changed the lower edge of the sleeves to a pleated frill to take full advantage of the plaid fabric. This change was partly inspired by the highly decorated cuffs in the early 1870s Day Dress in Striped Silk/Cotton shown in *Patterns of Fashion 2*, by Janet Arnold (2022, p. 33). There is also the general use of flounces in the 1870s, described in Lisa Hodgkins' *Everyday Fashion in Found Photographs*. "Fashions adorned with flounces (ruffles) were typical of the early 1870s" (2022, p. 74) (Fig. 4.22).

Fig. 4.22 This brown walking dress is a wonderful example of an early 1870s bustle style. Public domain.

I did not include boning in my bodice, but I did add a waist stay after the first wear to help keep it in the proper position. Images of waist stays within extant bodices abound (Arnold, 2022, p. 35, p. 39, p. 41), but I ended up turning to a book aimed at modern vintage sewists for instructions (Hirsch, 2016, p. 91). Happily, the same technique used to hold up a 1950s-style strapless cocktail dress also works very well to keep the back of my 1870s bodice from riding up as I walk.

I could have used Janet Arnold's diagrams to create my skirt, overskirt, and even a few of my accessories, but I was concerned that trying to use her work for the first time in this project might set me up to run beyond the limits of both my fabric and skill. So, I based my skirt and overskirt on the patterns in *Making Victorian Costumes for Women* by Heather Audin (2022, p. 91). Audin's book is aimed at the amateur hobbyist who has some experience in dressmaking. She has left some methods, such as how to finish a skirt hem, up to the reader. Her instructions are clear, and many photographs in the text also help guide the way. Her work as a museum curator probably motivated her concise summaries of fashion trends. I find her explanation of the differences between the first bustle (late 1860s to mid-1870s) and second bustle (most of the 1880s) styles very clear and helpful.

I am not sure if everyone could have made the bodice, skirt, and overskirt out of the amount of fabric I had, but my short stature allowed me to save enough fabric when I made the skirt to be able to make the overskirt. I underlined the back of the overskirt in silk organza to give it more body, and I lined it in scraps from other projects simply because I was out of fabric.

The skirt does have a short train. For my own sense of safety, comfort, and degree of not wanting to add to my laundry pile, I have added some small hooks and eyes to the back of the skirt so that I can avoid dragging it on the ground.

Chemisette and Sleeves

In her pattern notes for the Early Bustle Era Basic Bodice, Marna Jean Davis writes that the square neckline can be worn as-is for the evening but should be paired with a chemisette for day wear. Janet Arnold includes pattern diagrams for what she calls a "detachable gilet[10] front and undersleeves" to go with the early 1870s Day Dress to make it "suitable for morning wear" (2022, p. 96). I was nearly completely out of the plaid fabric, so I decided to sew a chemisette and a set of undersleeves in white cotton using a Truly Victorian pattern.

Other Accessories

I have purchased a purse, gloves, hats, a satin-lined fake fur muff, and some hairpieces to complete my look for Polly. Just as with my modern wardrobe, I may never be truly finished adding pieces here and there, as I find them.

The 1870s ensemble, as I wear it in 2024, cost us about $105 in sewing patterns, $425 in fabric, and $400 in purchased garments, not accounting for accessories such as hats and gloves, since those change based on the season and if I plan to be outdoors.

I find the ensemble no more uncomfortable or restrictive than any other formal dress with a long skirt. If I plan to drive a car, it is easier if I remove my bustle and loosen the ties of my corset. During a very cold Minnesota winter, I would consider adding long underwear as my first layer, but that is true no matter what.

5
Living anti-racist history and opening the archives

"Come sit on the floor, I want to braid your hair. You have such good hair."[11]

It was 1994. I was a freshman in high school and completely devoted to the older students, who I looked up to as mature and sophisticated. Flattered that she considered my waist-length, not-blonde, not-raven hair to be "good," I obediently sat on the floor in front of a sophomore whose name I no longer remember, handing her my hairbrush so she could work on my post-gym, damp head.

Tears sprang to my eyes and rolled down my face as she yanked on my scalp. I had thought I had signed up for a gentle hair brushing and a firm French braid. The single hair tie I wore on my wrist was clearly not going to fit my self-appointed stylist's ambitions.

"Um, I thought you were just braiding my hair?" I tentatively protested.

"I am! Dang, it's slippery. You don't have any pomade? Are you tender headed? Don't be tender headed." She scolded me, snapping open a packet of tiny elastic bands.

"I don't know what that is, but can't you make the braids looser?" I whined, reaching up to pat my sore head.

"No, and don't scratch! Wear a scarf to bed and these will stay in a while." She kept working. It felt like it took hours, but lunch was only 45 minutes, so it was probably the pain telescoping my memory.

I was too embarrassed to say I didn't have any idea how a scarf would help my hairstyle, since I only wore wool scarves around my neck in the coldest weather. Decades before I would hear the term, "cultural appropriation," I wore my hair in six fat cornrow-style braids for about 24 hours.

When my mother came home from work that night, she reminisced about her job as a public school teacher in the 1970s. Some students would pat and touch her hair out of curiosity.

The style was short-lived. The next lunch hour was spent with three sophomores undoing the previous day's work because the braids weren't holding. My relatively straight, fine hair was working its way out of the braids, making me look somewhat like Pinhead from the Hellraiser movies. "We can't have you walking around looking like a demon."

Years later, I recounted this story, sitting in my living room with my hair dressed in pomade and powder, styled over a wool-stuffed pillow to Marie Antoinette heights. I was hosting a make and take party with friends. Following the instructions in The

American Duchess Guide to 18th Century Beauty, we made personalized beauty products and discussed the history of the "frizzed" hair trend of the late eighteenth century. Although able to extemporaneously explain the physics and chemistry behind the melting, tempering, and whipping steps for creating the styling products, I needed Cheyney McKnight's words (Stowell et al., 2019, pp. 156–157) to grasp the sartorial link between this specific hairstyle and enslavement. My friends gently teased me about my tender head and my former deep ignorance about sleep bonnets.

Living "vintage style, not vintage values"

Dressing in public in historic ensembles, especially when you've had the time, energy, and privilege to do it "correctly," is a *blast*. It seems everyone you see is delighted to see you. For an extrovert with social anxiety, it's an effective way to get a lot of positive attention from people who would otherwise walk right past you. I was originally motivated to make and wear eighteenth-century-style clothes because I saw someone dressed beautifully at a Mount Vernon 4th of July weekend in 2017. My nearly 5-year-old saw how I admired the woman and said, "Mamma, do you like that? You could *make* that!"

To celebrate my 40th birthday in 2019, I rented a house at Colonial Williamsburg, invited friends to a brunch-and-get-dressed party in the sitting room, and went on a promenade with a large group, all dressed in late eighteenth-century-style clothes. I wore my first riding habit and an absolutely enormous hat and wig.

Visiting eighteenth-century-styled sites in period-appropriate clothes was a fun hobby that seemed perfectly innocent, despite the occasional shocks I felt when people spoke casually of "fighting Indians" or "merciless red savages."

In 2021, it seemed like a storm that had been gathering over the eighteenth-century segment of the historic costuming hobby broke. This was an illusion, since black, brown, and indigenous costume and fashion history enthusiasts had been speaking up about their marginalization on social media platforms for years. The conversation about appropriate places and times to wear eighteenth-century-style dress as a guest at historic sites while paid staff provided live interpretation and guest interaction was partially overshadowed by the obvious reservations of non-white people about participating in the American Civil War interpretation community.

Cheyney McKnight started her thought-provoking posts on Instagram in late 2014, reflecting on the balances and strains of Black Americans working in historic interpretation, including thoughtful reflections on her experiences working at Colonial Williamsburg. In 2018, a group including Vivien of Fresh Frippery attended a large costume arts conference in Los Angeles as a group dressed as Edwardian maids. Vivien Lee's Instagram post about the event was captioned,

> "Happy and serious Downton Abbey maids on the third day of Costume College. We often get called by each other's names at costume events so we decided to match and confuse everyone who thinks all Asians look alike. If you find one of us and name us correctly you will get a special button!" (Lee, 2018).

Posts and conversations like this started to gain momentum in the larger, white-dominated community. As early as March of 2019, the band leader and entertainer Dandy Wellington sold enameled lapel pins reading "Vintage Style, not Vintage Values." He focuses on the aesthetic of the 1920s and 1930s, but the message is applicable to all eras marked by widespread, racialized oppression.

The 2021 Juneteenth commemorations must have been planned at Colonial Williamsburg long in advance of the federal adoption of the holiday on June 17, 2021. The weekend's program included a keynote address, a cookout, and the live performance of a play, "*Loquacious Lucy*, the story of an enslaved child who learns her friend has been sold" (The Colonial Williamsburg Foundation, 2021).

During and directly after the weekend, controversy broke in the eighteenth-century-historic-costuming corner of Instagram, Facebook, and YouTube. Why? Because a group of parasocially acquainted hobbyists gathered on the site and held a picnic near these outdoor events, drawing interest from fellow patrons. In short, a group of beautifully dressed people visibly celebrating across from the Governor's Mansion pulled focus from the hard work of the paid staff to represent difficult topics, including oppression, enslavement, and racialized violence. This gave visitors who didn't want to engage with such difficult topics an attractive alternative (personal communication, unnamed source, 30 November 2024).

Encouraging paying guests to enjoy historic-style clothes against the backdrop of a lovingly recreated eighteenth-century town is part of the business of Colonial Williamsburg. The site hosts a thriving trade in eighteenth-century clothes at the Tarpley, Thompson & Company Store and sells reproduction cotton prints by the yard in all gift shops and online. Nothing the patrons were doing violated the policies of the site or attracted formal censure from the staff. But disrespect is disrespect, and many people with deep commitments to the site took sides and pointed fingers, both in person and online.

In short, it is possible to create harm and distress among living people through wearing historic clothes in public, even without meaning to do so. Following the blowback, several high-profile Instagram accounts made public apologies and even made vows to stop "dressing out" when not formally part of a museum program.

Booker T. Washington High School, Greenwood, Black lives matter, and Juneteenth

We joined this discussion with an unusual level of exposure to Black history and discourse, at least in terms of our hometown and our historically African-American high school, Booker T. Washington in Tulsa, Oklahoma.

> "Founded in 1913 to serve the citizens of the African-American community, Booker T. Washington was chosen in 1973 to be the vehicle for Tulsa's school desegregation program. This school was established as a magnet school and serves students from every racial, ethnic, religious, and socio-economic group in Tulsa. Booker

T. Washington continues to thrive based on the twin ideals of promoting excellence and acceptance of diversity. This philosophy has resulted in our institution's recognition as one of the most successful secondary schools in the United States. Our student body boasts a nationally-ranked academic bowl team and speech and debate team, as well as championship basketball, football, soccer, swim, and volleyball teams" (Booker T. Washington High School, 2024).

In the late 1990s, students always referred to the high school as "Booker T." We engaged fully in the campus life of this Black-first space. We learned slang we 100 percent knew not to actually use, enthusiastically participated in school-wide drum major dances, and celebrated Juneteenth alongside our classmates.

"In early 1921, Tulsa's Greenwood district had become a prosperous, family-oriented, autonomous Black community of more than 10,000 people…one of the wealthiest black communities… possibly in the United States of America" (Fletcher and Howard, 2023, p. xxii). On May 31, 2021, the Greenwood district was utterly destroyed. "Survivors of the massacre and their descendants estimate…possibly as many as 3,000 [people were killed] …buried in mass graves…thrown in the [Arkansas] river, or perished in homes and businesses burned beyond recognition…" (Fletcher and Howard, 2023, p. xxiv).

Today, there's even a YouTube video from Extra History about the destruction of North Tulsa if you prefer to get your history through the medium of animation (Extra History, 2020). The 100-year anniversary of the massacre encouraged memorials and discussions. A few remaining survivors have recently been supported in speaking out. Viola Ford Fletcher, seven years old at the time, recounted a scene straight from a living nightmare: "An airplane flew above us dropping firebombs. Men tossed torches from the street into the windows of people's homes. The buildings were burning from both top and bottom, all at once. Ash was falling on the trees like snow" (Fletcher and Howard, 2023, p. 9).

But at the start of our freshman year of high school, many of these voices had been silenced or pushed out of the narrative for more than seventy years. When the issue did come up, terms like "riot" and "mob" were still being used to suggest the disorganized crime of a handful of armed citizens. The *Oklahoma Commission to Study the Tulsa Race Riot of 1921* would not begin its work until our senior year. The final report would not be released until 2001.

The continued architectural desolation of North Tulsa in the mid-1990s even hums in the background of our classmate Benjamin Lytal's 2013 novel, *A Map of Tulsa*. His fictional main character, walking through a simulacrum of the real downtown of Tulsa, comments: "Isn't Tulsa weird…on that side of the tracks, we build up all the skyscrapers, but immediately on this side of the tracks it's nothing but a warehouse district" (pp. 6–7).

North Tulsa's relative emptiness wasn't weird or accidental. It was demolished and figuratively sown with salt.

We didn't know the whole story, but we weren't as ignorant as the imaginary Jim Praley. With all this bubbling under the surface, we benefited from the words of Dale Watts, Marvin Battle, and Rick Arrington. Mr. Watts was not a history teacher but an

English teacher. He displayed unabashed love of the work of Ralph Ellison and Toni Morrison, reading passages aloud with dramatic gusto, really chewing on the words, playing jazz records, and linking these works to the broader context of the Harlem Renaissance and the Great Migration. He made a habit of describing how the North Tulsa we knew was the rubble of a once large and extremely wealthy community.

Our unusually deep education on the Oklahoman Black experience had gaps. We assumed many of the people who settled north of the Frisco Railroad tracks had made a journey from the Deep South during reconstruction or in the following decades, during the Great Migration.

Rick Arrington and Marvin Battle, as you would expect of history teachers, thoroughly explained reconstruction and the development of Oklahoma statehood. They neglected to mention enslavement among the Tribes except in the context of the Civil War era alliances of the Tribes. Or maybe they did, and I wasn't ready to hear it.

The puff pieces in the Tulsa World newspaper, describing the Brady Theater as haunted, joined our hometown with many other local legends, safely bricking up the sins of our collective past among impotent, disembodied spirits. As Tiya Miles noted in her book *Tales from the Haunted South: Dark Tourism and the Memories of Slavery from the Civil Rights Era*, "Because modern culture dismisses the possibility of ghosts…revelations of historical import embedded in ghost stories are therefore dismissed as unreal" (2015, p. 15).

Walking the walk

Simply "being" anti-racist is not enough. Acknowledging the harms of enslavement as a footnote is not enough. Being well-meaning allies wasn't enough: we had work to do.

If you think, "I can't do anything," you have been misinformed.

You can educate yourself about the widespread contributions of enslaved people and their descendants to American society, often in spite of the majority culture's best efforts to shut them out. Especially if you "love history." Double if you love to dress up like the people who were enslavers or benefited from the hierarchy that long-term chattel enslavement required.

Ask questions about your received family story, if you have one. The "family tree" style websites are interesting, but they're often run and populated by family history fandoms, not researchers. And they're big business: monetizing people's interest in "who they are" and adding layers to the veneer of inherited talent, importance, and nationalism.

Here's what we do to support living people both in person and virtually.

Lisa recounts:

> A glance at the references we used to write this book will show that I spent a lot of time with the records of the National Archives in 2022-2024. In 2022, my engagement with the materials was entirely virtual. In 2023, I had saved up some annual leave and figured I would like to personally help the Archives increase the availability of

Living anti-racist history and opening the archives 167

records virtually. Confident I would pass a background check, I wrote this email on August 21:

Dear Innovation Hub :

I would like to schedule a visit to the Innovation Hub on October 3, 2023 to work as a citizen scanner.

If possible, I would prefer to scan enrollment jackets from the Final Rolls of the Five Civilized Tribes, 1899–1914, NAID : 617283

If that's not possible, I'd like to scan pension files of Indian Scouts and Buffalo Soldiers.

Please let me know what I should do in advance to participate.

Sincerely,

Lisa Neel

The response arrived in my inbox about 90 business minutes later. It read, in part,

"I have put you on the schedule for Tuesday, October 3. Unfortunately, the enrollment jackets from the Final Rolls have not been approved for scanning in the Hub. We do have plenty of Indian Scout and Buffalo Soldier pensions, though, so I'll make sure that there are some available for you. Thank you for scanning!"

Six weeks later, I crossed Pennsylvania Avenue, NW, and reported to the National Archives Innovation Hub. It's a welcoming, comfortable space, but they have normal Federal Building security measures in place: I presented my bag for search, emptied my pockets, and walked through a metal detector before finding a locker for my purse and water bottle.

No purses or bags are allowed in the scanning room, so I brought a small coin purse to hold my locker key, my research card, and some extra change.

Some of the papers I scanned were more than 120 years old. This is work that requires bare, clean human hands to unfold, position, and carefully replace. Some light, thin folders had dozens of pieces of paper as thin as an onion skin. The actual scanning isn't difficult work. There's a little "hurry up and wait," but you get to really read these documents, which generally add up to a story told backward.

Working as a historical document scanner is surprisingly intimate. These records don't quite have the deep humanity of antique garments as described lovingly by textile curators like Brandon Brooks of Genesee Country Museum (Brooks, 2024). But in handling each form, note, and letter, you feel the different quality of paper available to the people that made the records, see where people crossed things out, or their pen blotted. Smears, fingerprints (both intentional and accidental), and "marks" are all there. Some documents have wax seals, tape, glue, or straight pins stuck into them.

On October 3, 2023, and December 7, 2023, I scanned hundreds of pages related to the work of the US Army during the Indian Wars (National Archives Catalog. Files Scanned by Lisa Neel, citizen archivist, 2024). I felt a little conflicted about working to distribute and honor these records, especially when the texts included descriptions of battles with Native Nations and documented the choices to join the military of four different men. As a Native person, it was just plain weird to handle an original of the Department of the Interior form 4-337 printed by the US government in 1917, bearing the information detailing the service records and petition for pension of Charles Henry. He was an Indian scout who served under General Custer with "Occupation at Enlistment" as: "Nothing. Living as an Indian" (National Archives Catalog, SO-13829, p. 125). Mr. Henry was dragged by his horse during a drill in 1874. The resulting injuries caused him lifelong disability but may have saved his life in the long run. He outlived Yellow Hair by at least four decades.

When you have been soothed by the office setting, library quiet, warmly welcoming guards, and 1940s-style sign on the wall reminding you that, "THIS IS YOUR HERITAGE," reading paper after paper reminding you that the Indian Wars were just another piece of war business to the US Army is jarring.

To be fair, I was also rattled by descriptions of serious injuries taken while falling from horses. I had a horse ride scheduled after my second scanning day and found myself reading several depositions from physicians of injuries some of these men suffered while taking involuntary dismounts from horseback.

I told myself that these scouts, soldiers, and teamsters deserved to have their records available to their descendants and researchers, just as I have for some of my ancestors. I encourage anyone that can take the time to consider volunteering at an archive near them. Additionally, anyone with an internet connection can train to be a citizen archivist: tagging and transcribing documents that are really, sincerely, not machine-readable.

Not your Mamma's history and Cheyney McKnight's Afrofuturism

Cheyney McKnight is a historian, thought leader, and performance artist based in New York City. Her public work focuses on first-person history interpretation and Afrofuturism. Her words have been a central part of my process of educating myself: enjoying her lectures and writing as a trusted source and being careful not to expect her to debate her points or offer her personhood up for debate. Luckily for me, she offers a parasocial window into her work on a global level through the *Not Your Mamma's History* Patreon account.

I wanted to be more active in her work than just supporting her as a patron. I participated as a seamstress in the Pinkster Sew Along of 2024, coordinated by Cheyney in partnership with the fabric and notions merchant Burnley and Trowbridge. It was my first time working with African wax print cotton, a fabric with a rich and interesting story all by itself. I was delighted when I opened the package and found that I had been assigned a fabric with a beautiful, complex design featuring my high school mascot colors of orange and black.

In 2022, Cheyney McKnight's writing alerted me to the work of the Slave Dwelling Project. I eagerly pre-ordered Mr. Joseph McGill's book when it came out in 2023. I wanted to avoid putting him in the position of being a referee or a confessor (McGill, Jr., and Frazier, 2023, p. 291), but I watched for an opportunity to engage with his ambitious, interesting project.

In October of 2024, I attended the *Slave Dwelling Project Conference: The Illusion of Freedom: Slavery in the Northern States*. Leading up to the event, I wasn't sure what to expect. Characteristically, I calmed my anxiety by focusing on what I was going to *wear* and finding people I knew speaking on the conference agenda. I hadn't gone to any large indoor events since early 2020, and I was anxious about being in a crowd in general, much less with an imaginary "E" on my chest for "I not only *look like* a honkey: I am descended from ENSLAVERS."

I made dinner plans with a few people, decided to tour the Franklin Print Shop museum with a copy of the Cherokee Phoenix, and packed a few hand sewing projects. I realized as I drove to Philadelphia that I had only been to public health conferences and tribal Gatherings of Nations, in which it is typical to see at least five people in any one room with knitting, beading, sewing, or quillwork in their hands. Do people do crafts at history conferences? I was going to find out.

Registration was at the host hotel, a few blocks from mine, and started at 8 a.m. sharp. As I walked downhill, the day's first cup of tea in my hand, Cheyney McKnight turned the corner on her way up that hill. I was very happy that the first person I met in this unfamiliar environment was a friend. We greeted each other; she reassured me that it would not be disrespectful to quietly hand sew in the corner, and I walked with more confidence toward a three-day agenda packed with titles such as "Descendants of Northern Slavery History, Black and White, Discuss Freedom and Resistance through the Lens of our Interconnected Family Legacies," "The Past is Not the Past: Understanding and Navigating the Historic Trauma of Slavery at Public Sites" and "Slaves Were the Commodity That Was Bought and Sold on Wall Street."

The conference was a blur of nearly hourly difficult choices. Every time slot had at least two things happening at once that sounded intriguing, and I didn't know enough about the field to choose presentations based on the reputation of each speaker. The atmosphere was energetic and engaging. Everyone seemed to be bursting with excitement about their work and connecting with each other: from seasoned academics to citizen archivists, middle school teachers, retired lawyers, genealogists, local historians, United States Park Service employees, activists, and journalists. In the brief gaps between sessions, my hand sewing had the intended effect of attracting strangers asking, "What are you making?" During sessions, I kept working so my hands were busy and my mouth could stay shut.

The presentations had standard PowerPoint decks, videos, and handouts just like any other professional conference. The hot water carafes were tainted with the taste of coffee, as is almost universally the case. When a speaker made an especially exciting point, a handful of audience members would murmur 'amen' or 'uh-huh!' This is a habit I grew up with but have suppressed since moving to the East Coast, and it was reviving to hear it.

Everyone seemed to have almost unlimited respect and positive regard for each other, even for an unknown outsider like me. I answered most questions about "What brings you here?" with a variation of "Cheyney McKnight turned me on to Joe McGill's work, and I wanted to learn." I found throughout the weekend that my attempts to downplay my own worth backfired. "I'm just a public health professional with a degree in microbiology" earned me responses ranging from, "So you're a genius!" to "Can you come speak to my students?"

I was determined to keep my focus on the work I was there to hear about by politely turning the conversation back to the presentations. I started to relax on the second day and explained my specific interests to a few people. Since moving away from Oklahoma, I have learned to disassociate briefly while people go through the micro-expressions that come with the dawning realization that I'm a light-skinned Cherokee, a person that popular culture has told them doesn't exist. They usually register confusion, uncertainty, surprise, then excitement or enthusiasm. I had to use this skill a few times over the weekend when my personal background came up, but no one doubled down, said anything negative, or slapped me on the back for being an "ally" to my own community when I confirmed, "I'm not *descended* from Cherokees, I'm a voting *citizen*." I never felt compelled to open my wallet and slap down my Cherokee Nation identity card. No white-coded people held their forearms next to mine to compare complexions. This self-selected group of people was unusually well primed to accept my complex identity without comment.

Lara had told me that all authors are thrilled to sign their books, but I'm always worried I'm bothering people when I ask for an inscription. Nevertheless, I arrived at the conference with my hardback copies of *Sleeping with the Ancestors* by Joe McGill and

Herb Frazier and *Black AF History* by Michael Harriot, hoping to meet at least one of them. I ended up running into Joe in the hallway on the second day. He was so delighted that he ran down the hall to catch his co-author for a second signature. He returned to get a selfie with me and ask:

"Have you read the book?"

"Um, yes…I'm going to use it as a reference in my book."

"Oh, what's your book about?"

"Cherokee women's dress history."

"What's that now?" He straightened up and looked me right in the eyes. I had his attention.

"Um…my ancestor lived from 1820 to 1872, and in researching her context I found that the family had enslaved people. I didn't know what to do about that. This is part of what I'm doing, I guess. I'm not sure what to do."

"Well, just remember the ancestors. I look forward to reading your book."

I felt more comfortable approaching Michael Harriot, since there was a specific book signing event, and I was second in line with my copy.

"Who do I make it out to?"

"Um, Lisa, like this name tag. I really enjoyed your book." I had planned to say something more original, but I was still recovering emotionally from his keynote address in which he passionately argued that while race *is* a social construct, it's still real and that all of America is "a Slave Dwelling."

"Nice, nice. What did you think?"

"I was impressed with your analysis of the interconnectedness of enslavement to the whole country. I think it mirrors the Cherokee experience and I plan to reference your comments in my book."

Apparently, I had recovered enough to come up with something interesting to say.

There were no microexpressions. Mr. Harriot's face lit up with an expression I think of as "journalist senses a lede."

"So you're…Cherokee?"

"Yes, and I'm researching the context of my ancestor who lived from 1820 to 1872. She died at the family mill." What is wrong with me? Why do I keep *leading* with that? It freaks people out.

"Did they…was this in Georgia?" His eyes seemed to get even brighter.

"Yes. Well, some of them started in Georgia. Then they survived the removal and rebuilt in Indian Territory and…" I looked to my left. A line was forming.

"We should talk about this some other time." He said, shaking my hand.

I was reeling again. Shocked that these scholars and journalists were taking me seriously. I had a long drive home that night, so I said my goodbyes to the people I had met, gave away the rest of my business cards, and left.

Wearing the dress: Finding and creating appropriate venues for dressing Polly

All this context was essential in our plans for how best to find and create appropriate venues for Dressing Polly. The first rule has always been: be sure your presence in historic dress is welcomed or otherwise allowed by the site.

Our general behavior while dressed as Polly follows the rules recently formalized by the Maryland Renaissance Faire.

In short: don't take up space you're not welcomed in, don't interrupt or disrupt the work of paid staff, and do be respectful of the site and other visitors.

We started the work while still relatively cloistered in separate pandemic-informed bubbles with our "Why It Matters" video series. Originally in a second-person, podcast-type format, we took turns presenting the research we had done to date on the family story and context. The research and writing for those videos eventually grew into the basis for this book.

Once we each had one Polly ensemble complete, we started looking for places where it made sense to "be" Polly outside of a photography studio.

Lara recounts. On July 1, 2023, the Alexander Ramsey House in St. Paul, Minn., held a reopening celebration. The house had been closed to the public for over three years. According to the Minnesota Historical Society's website, the 1872 house is "one of the best-preserved Victorian homes in the world, filled with over 14,000 original family objects and furnishings." (Minnesota Historical Society, 2024b)

Excited to visit, I bought tickets for myself and my wife. I emailed the event organizer to make sure my history-themed dress would be acceptable, and they answered that I was welcome to dress as I liked. I dressed as Polly; my wife came in everyday clothes. It was a hot, lovely day, but visiting the home of the first governor of Minnesota as a Native American person is not without its moments of dissonance. He was also a superintendent of Indian affairs and a key player in the signing of treaties that either ceded or stole, depending on your perspective, 24 million acres of Dakota land in 1851. After an armed conflict with the Dakota in 1862, Ramsey made a passionate call for the removal of the Dakota from Minnesota, saying, "The…Indians of Minnesota must be exterminated, or driven forever beyond the borders of the state" (Minnesota Historical Society, 2024a).

For perspective on those 24 million acres, the whole of Minnesota is a little over 51 million acres (Minnesota DNR, 2024).

While much more grand than any home Polly is likely to have entered in her lifetime, the house is a stunning example of historical preservation and truly allows visitors to feel as if they are stepping back into the past (Minnesota Historical Society, 2024b).

Lisa recounts. It was a hot, muggy day in August of 2023 when I first pulled into the parking lot at Colvin Run Mill. The grist mill, built about 1811, is now owned by the Fairfax County Park Authority. Set in gorgeously landscaped grounds, the mill is one of the last of its kind still functional, and the volunteers and staff run it using water power every other Sunday, April through October (Fairfax County, 2023). The entire site slopes toward the mill. The red brick building looked more solid than the photographs of the Beck-Hildebrand mill ruins I had found in my research (Fig 1.1 and Mill Pictures.com, 2024). The silhouette roughly matched the family mill as depicted in the Vinson Lackey painting of 1945 (Gilcrease, 2024): three ranks of full windows set into a peaked roof.

The shiver of memory and goosebumps I felt when I first heard the throbbing purr of the grinding millstones gave way to a little laugh at myself. "Maybe milling is in the blood…but probably this just reminds me of the whooshing sound of amplified gestational ultrasounds." I tried to capture the background noise with the little microphone built into my cell phone, but it came out tinny and muffled. If you ever get the chance to stand in a nineteenth-century mill while it operates, the whole building gently vibrates, and the sound is like a huge cat purring in slow playback.

I made that visit wearing modern clothes, unsure if the site would be safe for someone in floor-length skirts or welcoming of respectful visitors wearing historic clothes. Visitors are kept well out of the way of the equipment. I peeked into the historic Miller's house, bought some freshly ground flour, and laid plans to return and contribute to the site's interpretation of nineteenth-century life. Later that year, I visited again for a themed event as a guest, this time dressed in my 1845 tear dress after checking with the site manager for their policy on guests wearing historic clothes. The event coordinator was thrilled to see me and welcomed me warmly. A brief chat led to several emails and phone calls, which led to a delightful afternoon teaching wool preparation and yarn spinning in the shadow of the miller's house the following spring and autumn. My relationship has developed with this site, allowing me to teach spinning to their employees, discuss their interpretation of enslavement at the site, and exchange bread recipes.

6
Honoring Polly Beck

Carol Hanisch's feminist paper, *The Personal is Political*, was written in a specific time and place, namely, the United States in 1969 (2009). The concept wrapped up so succinctly in that title has left its original context behind to the point of banality in modern discourse. This is, perhaps, a testament to the chord it strikes, although the authors encourage everyone to read the original paper. At this writing, it is freely available on Hanisch's website.

If the personal is political, so is history. Whose history is worth telling? Who gets to tell it?

Polly's story is deeply personal to us, not just because she is our ancestor, but because women like her were the links that kept Cherokee identity alive during major historical events and the attempted destruction of the Cherokee people. When Polly traveled from her homeland to Indian Territory, she crossed an international border. In modern language, she may not have been a refugee, but she was certainly a migrant. Her family had some degree of choice in the exact timing and nature of their immigration, but they could not have chosen to stay. She, and all of the other Cherokee people who did not find ways to remain behind, had been collectively expelled by the United States.

Polly may or may not have been a refugee during the Civil War. Many were. In any case, she survived these two upheavals, built her business, raised her family, and then was shot and killed by a man when she was in her early 50s. She only lived to see one of her grandchildren born. It should have been more.

If the authors had an unbroken oral history to tell, they would certainly have been telling it as long as they could talk. Our family loves stories, and, like many, we have our favorites of good times, funny moments, and struggles that have been overcome. Five generations is a long time for one person's story to live, and it's possible that Julia Ann, who lost her mother and first husband to this cluster of violence in 1872, didn't encourage the telling of the story because it brought her pain.

In the absence of an unbroken chain of storytellers—daughter to son to grandchild—Lara and Lisa have chosen to understand Polly's life by exploring the aspects of it that are available to them. Without a ready-made narrative, they research. Without a ready-made image, they re-create how Polly might have looked. In doing so, their hope is to show the world that Cherokee people are, and have always been, storytellers who speak and live in the moment of their time.

Polly's untimely death linked her forever with two interdependent and ongoing struggles: the boundaries of tribal sovereignty and safety for indigenous women. While her death may not have been gendered violence as we currently understand it, the ambiguous jurisdictional cobweb experienced by Cherokee citizens in Indian Territory which led to a federal posse interrupting Cherokee court proceedings in Goingsnake, has never been fully resolved. The liminal nature of indigenous women's safety has led to awareness efforts including the REDress Project and Missing and Murdered Indigenous Women (Stewart, 2023).

> "Jaime Black, a Métis multidisciplinary artist and art mentor based in Winnipeg, Canada, created The REDress Project to give a platform to those women and girls now silent. In North America, Native women, girls and those who identify as women experience violence at far greater rates than those who are non-Indigenous" (Bolen, 2019).

These problems are unsolved but not intractable. We hope that our work on The Polly Beck Project will have a positive impact on awareness and action to improve how contemporary people think of history and the resilience, creativity, and complex legacy of Cherokee women: past, present, and future.

Recommended discussion questions

1. Does a person's skin tone affect your judgment of their racial identity? How is that affected by photographic technology and reproduction?
2. Were you surprised to learn that non-white groups of people sometimes actively participated in the enslavement of other people?
3. How might the images in museums and historical reenactments affect your approach to understanding history? How could people designing, casting, and recording reenactment events take care to avoid stereotypes?

Notes

1. Note should be taken here of the widespread variation to be found in the spelling of this important Cherokee family name. Patriarch of the family, according to Emmett Starr's History of the Cherokee Indians (1922), was John Hildebrand, a native of Germany. He had five children by his first wife, a German, and four by his second, Susannah Womancatcher, a Cherokee. Succeeding generations of large families produced a large number of Hildebrands, of varying degrees of Cherokee blood and a bewildering variety of spellings. Starr gives the genealogy of no less than 64 Hildebrands, with that spelling. Unfortunately, the 1835 Census of Cherokees taken before their removal to Indian Territory gives the name as Helderbrand, and the Final Rolls of the Cherokees, prepared in 1902, give it as Hilderbrand. Elsewhere in print are such additional spellings as Hilderbrandt, Helterbrand, and Hulderbrand. For what it's worth, the post office at the site—from August 3, 1866, to June 25, 1889—was Hilderbrand. Throughout this nomination, Hildebrand will be used in deference to Starr as a recognized genealogist. The decision should not be taken as either final or official (National Archives Catalog, 1972, p. 3).
2. Perdue notes that this name is also spelled "Kesterson" or "Chesterton." (Perdue, 1993, p. 39).
3. Not actually Native American, but that's another book.
4. Confusingly, drawers are sometimes called "bloomers" because they resemble the loose, ankle-length trousers of the Bloomer costume (Lynn, 2014, p. 220).
5. Whalebone is actually baleen (Lynn, 2014, p. 73).
6. Modern corset-wearers call this "Bunny Ears" lacing (The Creative Couture Studio, 2023).

7. If you are in the habit of gawking at corsets in museums and being concerned about their measurements, please remember that they were (and are) generally worn with a gap of about 2 to 4 inches in the back (Lynn, 2014, p. 73).
8. "Short-waisted" doesn't simply mean short of stature. It means there is less distance between the shoulder and the position of the waist (Talbot, 1943, p. 89). Modern readers might consider a short-waisted style to produce the effect of high-rise jeans as opposed to mid-rise or low-rise jeans.
9. John's father was Blacksoot (also known as Black Sut) Beck (National Archives Catalog, Card #6829). We discuss him more in Chapter 1 using his formal name, "Jesse Beck," although other records also give Surry Eaton Beck as his full name.
10. A "gilet" is a "sleeveless bodice shaped to imitate a man's waistcoat" (Cumming et al., 2010, p. 92), and Janet Arnold may be using it here because the garment she is describing has no collar and is made of fabric matching the bodice.
11. I was completely ignorant of the overall context of "good hair." In my defense, Chris Rock's documentary by this title was 15 years in the future.

References

Ancestry.com Operations, Inc. (2015). *Oklahoma, U.S., Wills and Probate Records, 1801–2008*. [online] Available at https://www.ancestry.com/search/collections/9077/ [Accessed 4 April 2024].

Amos, A. (2001). *The Alden Amos Big Book of Handspinning: Being a Compendium of Information, Advice, and Opinions on the Noble Art & Craft*. Loveland, Colorado: Interweave Press, Inc.

Arnold, J. (2022). *Patterns of Fashion 2: The Content, Cut, Construction and Context of Women's Dress c. 1860 – 1940 in English and French Collections*. London: The School of Historical Dress.

Audin, H. (2022). *Making Victorian Costumes for Women*. Ramsbury, Marlborough: The Crowood Press Ltd.

Baker, S., Boney, Jr., R., Ganteaume, C. and Tehee, C. (2018). *After Removal: Rebuilding the Cherokee Nation*. Canada: Helmerich Center for American Research at Gilcrease Museum.

Baker, T. and Baker, J. eds. (1996). *The WPA Oklahoma Slave Narratives* (Norman, OK: The University of Oklahoma Press).

Beck, J. Application Number 866. [Online] National Archives Catalog. Available at: https://catalog.archives.gov/id/56386244?objectPage=4 [Accessed 1 April 2024].

Bell, J. and Beck, S. (n.d.) "Address to the Citizens of the Cherokee Nation," John Ross Papers, Folder 1319, Thomas Gilcrease Institute for American Art and History, Tulsa, Okla. Available at: https://collections.gilcrease.org/object/3026269 [Accessed 5 February 2024].

Beveridge, S. (2011). Back to school special Part 2: Early literacy data. [Online] Available at: https://blog.oup.com/2011/09/literacy-data/#:~:text=The%20Census%20Bureau%20first%20reported,age%20of%2020)%20was%20literate. [Accessed 18 February 2024].

Blackburn, B. King, D. and Morton, N. (2018). *Cherokee Nation: A History of Survival, Self Determination, and Identity*. Tahlequah, OK: Cherokee Nation.

Bolen, A. (2019). A Place for the Taken: The REDress Project Gives a Voice to Missing Indigenous Women. [Online] Available at: https://www.americanindianmagazine.org/story/redress-project [Accessed 25 November 2024].

Booker T. Washington High School. (2024). *Booker T. Washington High School*. [Online] Available at: https://btw.tulsaschools.org/ [Accessed 1 May 2024].

Brooks, B (2024). Genesee Country Village & Museum 2024 Virtual Fashion History Series. [Online] Available at: https://www.gcv.org/event/virtual-lecture-series-introduction-to-19th-century-fashionvirtual-lecture-series/ [Accessed 23 November 2024].

Buffalo Wool Company (n.d.). *American Bison Apparel and Accessories: Field Tested Over 10,000 Years*. Brochure. Weatherford, TX. www.thebuffalowoolco.com

Boudinot, W. (1871). Godey's Lady's Book. *Cherokee Advocate* [Online] Vol. 1, No. 48, Ed. 1 Saturday, March 18, 1871. Available at: https://gateway.okhistory.org/ark:/67531/metadc1849367/ [Accessed 31 January 2024].

Carney, V. (2005). *Eastern Band Cherokee Women: Cultural Persistence in their Letters and Speeches*. Knoxville, TN: The University of Tennessee Press.

Case, M. (2012). *Simply Cherokee: Let's Learn Cherokee*. Bloomington, IN: Authorhouse.

Chandler, S. Application Number 868. [Online] Available at: https://catalog.archives.gov/id/56386260?objectPage=5 [Accessed 1 May 2024].

Cherokee.org. (2024). ᎣᏯ ᎠᎾᏞᏐᎢ ᏗᎦᏔᎳᏐRT: *Remember the Removal*. [Online] Available at: https://www.cherokee.org/about-the-nation/remember-the-removal/ [Accessed 7 April 2024].

Cherokee Phoenix. (2023a). *"We Are Cherokee" Freedmen exhibit closes*. [Online] Available at: https://www.cherokeephoenix.org/culture/we-are-cherokee-freedmen-exhibit-closes/article_e2439180-201c-11ee-a1bc-83e09acd3a56.html [Accessed 20 September 2024].

Cherokee Phoenix. (2023b). *Dec. 13 is declared Ruth Muskrat Bronson Day in the CN*. [Online] Available at: https://www.cherokeephoenix.org/news/dec-13-is-declared-ruth-muskrat-bronson-day-in-the-cn/article_4f5e9398-a009-11ee-923a-d3c3f5a13ff9.html [Accessed 14 April 2024].

Clark, E. (2009). *The Dressmaker's Guide: 1840 – 1865*. ESCPublishing.com

Clark, E. (2010). Judicious Padding: Making Bust Pads for Optimal Fit. [Online] The Sewing Academy. Available at: https://www.thesewingacademy.com/wp-content/uploads/2011/04/2010JudiciousPadding.pdf [Accessed 28 February 2024].

Clee, P. (2003). *Photography and the Making of the American West*. North Haven, CT: The Shoe String Press.

The Colonial Williamsburg Foundation (2021). Juneteenth Press Release [Online]. Available at: https://www.colonialwilliamsburg.org/documents/284/Juneteenth-press-release-2021-2.pdf [Accessed 10 October 2024].

The Colonial Williamsburg Foundation (2024). *Dress*. object number 1998-232 [Online] Available at: https://emuseum.history.org/objects/5603/dress;jsessionid=4F116F7E4991FD03E6BC2B7CFADF16F5 [Accessed 2 March 2024].

Confer, C. (2007). *The Cherokee Nation in the Civil War*. Norman, OK: The University of Oklahoma Press.

Conley, R. (2005). *The Cherokee Nation: A History*. Albuquerque, NM: University of New Mexico Press.

The Creative Couture Studio. (2023). *How to Lace a Corset-Bunny Ears-Self Lacing Method*. [video] Available at: https://www.youtube.com/watch?v=PeqNkxzG82g [Accessed 3 March 2024].

Cumming, V., Cunnington, C. and Cunnington, P. (2010). *The Dictionary of Fashion History*. New York, NY: Berg.

Cunnington, C. and Cunnington, P. (1959). *Handbook of English Costume in the Nineteenth Century*. London: Faber and Faber Limited.

Current, K. (1986). *Photography and the Old West*. New York, NY: Harry N. Abrams, Inc.

Daughters of the American Revolution. (2016). *An Agreeable Tyrant: Fashion After the Revolution*. Lanham, MD: Corporate Press.

Daughters of the American Revolution. *Corset* [Online] Available at: https://collections.dar.org/mDetail.aspx?rID=48.49.1%20%20%20%20%20%20%20%20%20%20%20%20&db=objects&dir=DARCOLL&osearch=Margaret%2520Johnson%2520Seeber&list=res&rname=&rimage=&page=1. [Accessed 27 February 2024].

Davis, M. (2015). *No Lady of Leisure: Clothing for the Victorian and Edwardian Working Woman*. https://www.marnajeandavis.com/

Dittman, W. (2018). Traditional Dress, Iconic Symbol. *Anadisgoi*. (summer/fall 2018) 35–36.

Dupuis, N. (2022). What your textbooks didn't tell you about Harriet Tubman. [Online] Available at: https://www.myeasternshoremd.com/dorchester_star/news/what-your-textbooks-didnt-tell-you-about-harriet-tubman/article_3dc6e470-acec-5432-8fc3-52ee5b2f040e.html [Accessed 1 June 2024].

Edwards, L. (2022). *Only the Clothes on Her Back: Clothing and the Hidden History of Power in the Nineteenth-Century United States.* New York, NY: Oxford University Press.

Extra History. (2020). The Burning of Black Wall Street – Tulsa, OK – Extra History [Online] Available at: https://www.youtube.com/watch?v=nc7IXBL9mng [Accessed 15 July 2020].

Fairfax County. (2023). Colvin Run Mill Historic Site. [Online] Available at: https://www.fairfaxcounty.gov/parks/colvin-run-mill/friends [Accessed 1 April 2023].

Fitzgerald, D. (2002). *Cherokee.* Portland, OR: Graphic Arts Center Publishing.

Fletcher, V. and Howard, I. (2023). *Don't Let Them Bury My Story: The Oldest Living Survivor of the Tulsa Race Massacre in Her Own Words.* New York, NY: Mocha Media Publishing.

Foreman, G. ed. (Microfilmed 1971) Typewrittten Copy of Census of 1835 of Cherokee Indians. [Online] Available at: https://www.okhistory.org/research/digital/foremantrans/foreman.sup14.pdf [Accessed 29 February 2024].

Lee, V. (2018). July 28, 2018. [Instagram]. Available at: https://www.instagram.com/p/BlyUWFCDsTG/?igsh=eGk3dGxoOXR6OHB0 [Accessed 28 July 2018].

Gabriel, R. (1941). *Elias Boudinot: Cherokee and His America.* Norman, OK: University of Oklahoma Press.

Gilcrease Museum. (2024). Beck Mill, Near Flint, 1838 / Vinson Lackey. [Online] Available at https://collections.gilcrease.org/object/011362. [Accessed 1 February 2021].

Gaul, T. ed. (2005. *To Marry an Indian: The Marriage of Harriett Gold and Elias Boudinot in Letters, 1823-1839.* Chapel Hill, NC: University of North Carolina Press.

Gibson, R. (2020). *The Corseted Skeleton: A Bioarchaeology of Binding.* Cham, Switzerland: Palgrave Macmillian.

Greene, S. (2014). *Wearable Prints, 1760-1860: History, Materials, and Mechanics*. Kent, Ohio: Kent State University Press.

Groom, G. ed. (2012). *Impressionism, Fashion, and Modernity*. Chicago, IL: The Art Institute of Chicago.

Hale, S. and Godey, L. eds. (1871a). Godey's Arm Chair. *Godey's Lady's Book*, [Online] Vol. 82, Iss. 491, (May 1871) Available at: https://babel.hathitrust.org/cgi/pt?id=umn.31951d00322056l&seq=457 [Accessed 1 February 2024].

Hale, S. ed. and Godey, L. ed. (1871b). Godey's Lady's Book. *Godey's Lady's Book*, [Online] Vol. 82, No. 491 (May 1871). Available at: https://archive.org/details/godeys.ladys.book.1871/page/n1/mode/2up [Accessed 1 February 2024].

Hanisch, C. (2009). The Personal is Political. [Online] Available at: https://www.carolhanisch.org/CHwritings/PIP.html [Accessed 28 July 2024].

Harjo, S. ed. (2014). *Nation to Nation: treaties between the United States and American Indian Nations*. Washington, DC: Smithsonian Institution.

Harris, K. ed. (2002). *Victorian Fashion in America: 264 Vintage Photographs*. Mineaola, NY: Dover Publications.

Harriot, M. (2023). *Black AF History: The Un-Whitewashed Story of America*. New York, NY: HarperCollins Books.

Hearst Corporation. *Harper's Bazaar*, [Online] Volume IV, Number 17 (April 29, 1871) Available at: https://reader.library.cornell.edu/docviewer/digital?id=hearth4732809_1425_018#page/15/mode/1up [Accessed 31 January 2024].

Higginbotham, A. (2018). *Not My Idea: A Book about Whiteness*. New York, NY: Dottir Press.

Hirsch, G. (2016). *Gertie's Ultimate Dress Book: A Modern Guide to Sewing Fabulous Vintage Styles*. New York, NY: STC Craft.

Hodgkins, L. (2022). *Everyday Fashion in Found Photographs: American Women of the Late 19th Century.* London: Bloomsbury Publishing.

Hogner-Weavel, Tonia. (2019). *Cherokee Clothing History and Resources.* Presentation on April 6, 2019. Tulsa, Oklahoma. Twins N Needles Vintage Sewing Adventure.

H.R. Exec. No. 287, 42nd Cong., 2nd Sess. Difficulties in Cherokee Country. Message from the President of the United States, in answer to a resolution of the House of the United States, in answer to a resolution of the House of Representatives of April 29, relative to the recent difficulties in the Cherokee Country. (1872) [Online] Available at: https://digitalcommons.law.ou.edu/cgi/viewcontent.cgi?article=3207&context=indianserialset [Accessed 29 February 2024].

JSTOR. (2024). Historical Relation of Facts Delivered by Ludovick Grant, Indian Trader, to His Excellency the Governor of South Carolina. The South Carolina Historical and Genealogical Magazine, Vol. 10, No. 1 (Jan., 1909), pp. 54–68 (15 pages) [Online] Available at: https://www.jstor.org/stable/27575222?seq=1 [Accessed 1 January 2024].

Justice, D. (2006). *Our Fire Survives the Storm: A Cherokee Literary History.* Minneapolis, MN: University of Minneapolis Press.

Kelton, P. (2015). *Cherokee Medicine, Colonial Germs: An Indigenous Nation's Fight against Smallpox, 1518–1824.* Norman: The University of Oklahoma Press.

Kelton, P. (2003). At the Head of the Aboriginal Remnant: Cherokee Construction of a "Civilized" Indian Identity During the Lakota Crisis of 1876. Great Plains Quarterly. [online] 23 (Winter 2003), 3–17. Available at: https://digitalcommons.unl.edu/greatplainsquarterly/2431 [Accessed 3 April 2024].

King, D. ed. (2007). *The Memoirs of Lt. Henry Timberlake: The Story of a Soldier, Adventurer, and Emissary to the Cherokees, 1756-1765.* Cherokee, NC: Museum of the Cherokee Indian Press.

King, T. (2013). *The Inconvenient Indian: A Curious Account of Native People in North America*. United States of America: Anchor Canada.

The Library Company of Philadelphia. *Accession Number 8421.F.2* [Online] Available at: https://digital.librarycompany.org/islandora/object/digitool%3A83047?solr_nav%5Bid%5D=26eee37c4b02811e926e&solr_nav%5Bpage%5D=0&solr_nav%5Boffset%5D=14 [Accessed 23 June 2024].

Lippard, L. ed. (1992). *Partial Recall*. New York, NY: The New Press.

Lynn, E. (2014). *Underwear: Fashion in Detail*. London: V&A Publishing.

Lytal, B. (2013, kindle edition). *A Map of Tulsa, A Novel*. Penguin Books.

Mankiller, W. (2004). *Every Day is a Good Day: Reflections by Contemporary Indigenous Women*. Golden, CO: Fulcrum Publishing.

Maryland Department of Natural Resources. American Indian Heritage Month at Fort Frederick October 31, 2017. [Online] Available at: https://news.maryland.gov/dnr/2017/10/31/american-indian-heritage-month-at-fort-frederick/ [Accessed 1 November 2017].

McCort, E. (2019). Maryland Center for History and Culture. [Online] Available at: https://www.mdhistory.org/truth-is-stranger-than-fictional-characters-dolly-varden-in-the-1870s/ [Accessed 10 March 2024].

McGill, Jr., J. and Frazier, H. (2023). *Sleeping with the Ancestors: How I Followed the Footprints of Slavery*. New York, NY: Hachette Books.

McLoughlin, W. (1984). *The Cherokee Ghost Dance: Essays on the Southeastern Indians 1789–1861*. United States of America: Mercer University Press.

McLoughlin, W. (1993). *After the Trail of Tears: The Cherokees' Struggle for Sovereignty 1839–1880.* Chapel Hill and London: The University of North Carolina Press.

Miles, T. (2010). *The House on Diamond Hill: A Cherokee Plantation Story.* Columbia: University of North Carolina Press.

Miles, T. (2015a). *Tales from the Haunted South: Dark Tourism and Memories of Slavery from the Civil War Era.* United States of America: University of North Carolina Press.

Miles, T. (2015b). *Ties That Bind: The Story of an Afro-Cherokee Family in Slavery and Freedom.* Oakland, California: University of California Press.

Mill Pictures.com (2024). Beck-Hildebrand Mill ruins. Available at: https://millpictures.com/mills.php?millid=1348 [Accessed April 1 2024].

Minneapolis Institute of Art (2023). *In Our Hands: Native Photography, 1890 to Now.* Minneapolis, MN: The Minneapolis Institute of Art.

Minnesota DNR. (2024). *Minnesota state land portfolio.* [Online] https://www.dnr.state.mn.us/slam/land-portfolio.html [Accessed 26 November 2024].

Minnesota Historical Society. (2024a). *Alexander Ramsey.* [Online] https://www.mnhs.org/ramseyhouse/learn/alexander-ramsey [Accessed 26 November 2024].

Minnesota Historical Society. (2024b). *Alexander Ramsey House.* [Online] https://www.mnhs.org/ramseyhouse [Accessed 26 November 2024].

Mooney, J. (2009) *Historical Sketch of the Cherokee*, third edition. Chicago, IL: Aldine Publications.

Mooney, J. (1902). *Myths of the Cherokee. Extract from the Nineteenth Annual Report of the Bureau of American Ethnology.* Washington, D.C.: Government Printing Office.

Nagle, R. (2024). *By the Fire We Carry: The Generations-Long Fight for Justice on Native Land*. New York, NY: HarperCollins Publishers.

National Archives Catalog. Dawes Enrollment Jacket for Cherokee, Cherokee by Blood, Card #6829. [Online] Available at: https://catalog.archives.gov/id/44770174?objectPage=3 [Accessed 29 February 2024]

National Archives Catalog. Dawes Enrollment Jacket for Cherokee, Cherokee by Blood, Card #6834. [Online] Available at: https://catalog.archives.gov/id/44770213 [Accessed 29 February 2024]

National Archives Catalog. Dawes Enrollment Jacket for Cherokee, Cherokee Freedmen, Card #186 (Nancy Sheppard). Applications for Enrollment in the Five Civilized Tribes, between 1898–1914. [Online] Available at: https://catalog.archives.gov/id/44907752 [Accessed 14 February 2023]

National Archives Catalog. Dawes Enrollment Jacket for Cherokee, Cherokee Freedmen, Card #294. (Rachel Ward) Applications for Enrollment in the Five Civilized Tribes, between 1898–1914. [Online] Available at: https://catalog.archives.gov/id/44908876 [Accessed 14 February 2023].

National Archives Catalog. Disapproved Pension Application File for Charles Henry, Indian Scouts, U.S. Army (SO-13829). [Online] Available at: https://catalog.archives.gov/id/346162019 [Accessed 21 September 2024]

National Archives Catalog. Eastern Cherokee Applications, August 29, 1906–May 26, 1909. [Online] Available at: https://catalog.archives.gov/id/301643 [Accessed 28 February 2024].

National Archives Catalog. Eastern Cherokee Applications, Application No. 859, between 1906–1909. [Online] Available at: https://catalog.archives.gov/id/56386147 [Accessed 28 February 2024].

National Archives Catalog. Files Scanned by Lisa Neel, citizen archivist. NAID numbers 351004929, 350903386, 346162019,

346167422 [Online] Available at: https://catalog.archives.gov/search?q=%22Lisa%20Neel%22 [Accessed 5 November 2024].

National Archives Catalog. National Register of Historic Places and National Historic Landmarks Program Records, 2013–2017. 1972. NAID: 86511065 [Online] Available at: https://catalog.archives.gov/id/86511065 [Accessed 1 April 2024].

National Archives Trust Fund Board, National Archives and Records Service, Washington, D.C. 1981. Eastern Cherokee Applications of the U.S. Court of Claims 1906–1909. [Online] Available at https://www.archives.gov/files/research/microfilm/m1104.pdf [Accessed 14 February 2024].

National Geographic Kids. (n.d.). Harriet Tubman, Spy. [Online] Available at: https://kids.nationalgeographic.com/history/article/harriet-tubman [Accessed 1 May 2024].

National Museum of African American History and Culture. Album With Previously Unknown Photo of Young Harriet Tubman To Go on Public View for the First Time [Online] Available at https://nmaahc.si.edu/about/news/album-previously-unknown-photo-young-harriet-tubman-go-public-view-first-time [Accessed 4 April 2024].

National Park Service (2016). [Online] Bison Bellows: Bison East of The Mississippi Available at: https://www.nps.gov/articles/bison-bellows-9-16-16.htm [Accessed 11 July 2024].

National Public Radio (2021). [Online] 3 Documentaries You Should Watch About The Tulsa Race Massacre Available at: https://www.npr.org/2021/05/30/1000923192/3-documentaries-you-should-watch-about-the-tulsa-race-massacre [Accessed 11 July 2024].

Naylor, C. (2008). *African Cherokees in Indian Territory: From Chattel to Citizens*. Chapel Hill, NC: The University of North Carolina Press.

Newton, S. (1974). *Health, Art and Reason: Dress Reformers of the 19th Century*. London: John Murray Ltd.

North, S. (2020). Indian Gowns and Banyans — New Evidence and Perspectives. *Costume* 54(1), pp. 30–55.

O'Dell, L. (n.d.). [Online] *Trail of Tears (Pageant)*. Available at: https://www.okhistory.org/publications/enc/entry?entry=TR004 [Accessed 7 April 2024].

Oklahoma Historical Society (2022). Email to Lisa Neel with subject line, *Research Request #7660 is complete.* 14 February.

Oklahoma Historical Society (2024a). [Online] *Hunter's Home History.* [Online] Available at: https://www.okhistory.org/sites/hhhistory [Accessed 30 January 2024].

Oklahoma Historical Society (2024b). Jennie Ross Cobb Collection. [Online] Available at: https://gateway.okhistory.org/search/?fq=str_title_serial:%22Jennie%20Ross%20Cobb%20Collection%22 [Accessed 30 January 2024].

Oklahoma Historical Society (2024c). Ozark & Cherokee Central Railroad. [Online] Available at: https://gateway.okhistory.org/ark:/67531/metadc1596685/ [Accessed 20 February 2024].

Olski, P. (2022). Dorset Buttons to Make. [Online] Piecework. Available at: https://pieceworkmagazine.com/dorset-buttons-make/ [Accessed 8 February 2024].

Parins, J. (2013). *Literacy and Intellectual Life in the Cherokee Nation, 1820–1906.* Norman, OK: University of Oklahoma Press.

Pate, J. (2010). "Cherokee Advocate," The Encyclopedia of Oklahoma History and Culture. [Online] Available at: www.okhistory.org/publications/enc/entry?entry=CH016. [Accessed 31 January 2024].

PBS. *The Civil War by the Numbers.* [Online] Available at: www.pbs.org/wgbh/americanexperience/features/death-numbers/ [Accessed 30 January 2024.]

Perdue, T. (1979). *Slavery and the Evolution of Cherokee Society, 1540–1866.* Knoxville, TN: University of Tennessee Press.

Perdue, T. (1993). *Nations Remembered: an oral history of the Cherokees, Chickaws, Choctaws, Creeks and Seminoles in Oklahoma, 1865 – 1907*. Norman, OK: the University of Oklahoma Press.

Perdue, T. ed. (1996). *Cherokee Editor: The Writings of Elias Boudinot*. Athens, GA: University of Georgia Press.

Perdue, T. (1998). *Cherokee Women: Gender and Culture Change, 1700–1835*. Lincoln, NE: University of Nebraska Press.

Perrot, P. (1994). *Fashioning the Bourgeoisie: A History of Clothing in the Nineteenth Century*. Princeton, NJ: Princeton University Press.

Postrel, V. (2020). *The Fabric of Civilization: How Textiles Made the World*. New York, NY: Basic Books.

Powell, J. (1887). *Fifth Annual Report of the Bureau of Ethnology to the Secretary of the Smithsonian Institution*. 1883–'84. Washington, DC: Government Printing Office.

Ramage, B. H. (1902). Georgia and the Cherokees. *The American Historical Magazine and Tennessee Historical Society Quarterly*, 7(3), (July, 1902), pp. 199–208. [Online] Available at: https://www.jstor.org/stable/42657252 [Accessed 20 January 2024].

Reid, J. (2006). *A Law of Blood: The Primitive Law of the Cherokee Nation*. DeKalb, Illinois: Northern Illinois University Press.

Rogers, M. (2010). *Delia's Tears: Race, Science, and Photography in Nineteenth-Century America*. New Haven, CT: Yale University Press.

Saini, A. (2019). *Superior: The Return of Race Science*. Boston, MA: Beacon Press.

Sandweiss, M. (2002). *Print the Legend: Photography and the American West*. New Haven, CT: Yale University Press.

Sartour. *Handwoven vintage linen fabric*. [Online] Available at: https://www.sartorbohemia.com/handwoven-vintage-linen-fabric-natural-100-linen_z16904/ [Accessed 28 February 2024].

Saunt, C. (2020). *Unworthy Republic: The Dispossession of Native Americans and the Road to Indian Territory.* New York, NY: W. W. Norton & Company.

Scott, C. Application Number 270. [Online] Available at https://catalog.archives.gov/id/56377816 [Accessed 1 May 2024].

Sears, R. (1969). 1902 Edition of *The Sears, Roebuck Catalog.* New York, NY: Bounty Books.

Senate Committee on Indian Affairs. "Testimony of Marilyn Vann, President of Descendants of Freedmen of the Five Civilized Tribes Association Presented to the United States Senate Committee on Indian Affairs, Oversight Hearing on Select Provisions of the 1866 Reconstruction Treaties Indian Affairs between the United States and Oklahoma Indian Tribes, July 27, 2022." [Online] Available at https://www.indian.senate.gov/wp-content/uploads/7%2025%202022%20%20Ms.%20Vann%20FINAL%20Freedman%20Testimony.pdf [Accessed 29 July 2024].

Severa, J. (1995). *Dressed for the Photographer: Ordinary Americans and Fashion, 1840–1900.* Kent, OH: The Kent State University Press.

Simonsen, J. (2006). *Making Home Work: Domesticity and Native American Assimilation in the American West, 1860–1919.* Chapel Hill, NC: The University of North Carolina Press.

Smithsonian American Art Museum. *International Indian Council (Held at Tallequah, Indian Territory, in 1843).* [Online] Available at: https://americanart.si.edu/artwork/international-indian-council-held-tallequah-indian-territory-1843-22854 [Accessed 8 February 2024].

Smithsonian National Museum of the American Indian. *Exhibit: Nation to Nation: Treaties Between the United States and American Indian Nations.* [Accessed 28 January 2024].

Smithsonian National Portrait Gallery. *David Rittenhouse NPG.98.73.* Available at: https://www.si.edu/object/npg_NPG.98.73 [Accessed 23 June 2024].

Smithsonian National Portrait Gallery. *John Quincy Adams.* Available at: https://npg.si.edu/object/npg_NPG.70.78?destination=node/63231%3Fedan_q%3D1843%2520president [Accessed 23 June 2024].

Smithsonian National Portrait Gallery. *John Ross – A Cherokee Chief.* Available at: https://npg.si.edu/object/npg_NPG.99.169.23?destination=node/63231%3Fedan_q%3Dcherokee%2520ross [Accessed 23 June 2024].

Smithsonian National Portrait Gallery. *Sequoyah (c. 1770–c. 1843).* Available at: https://npg.si.edu/learn/classroom-resource/sequoyah-c-1770%E2%80%93c-1843 [Accessed 23 June 2024].

Sontag, S. (1977). *On Photography.* New York, NY: Farrar, Straus and Giroux.

Starr, E. (1921). *History of the Cherokee Indians and Their Legends and Folk Lore.* Oklahoma City, Oklahoma: Warden Company.

Stewart, L. (2023). Missing and Murdered Indigenous Women and Girls: A Crisis Hiding in Plain Sight. [Online] Available at: https://www.culturalsurvival.org/news/missing-and-murdered-indigenous-women-and-girls-crisis-hiding-plain-sight?gad_source=1&gclid=CjwKCAiA3ZC6BhBaEiwAeqfvyiPxup8M2QZuHo6JNlvnjr5TKkJWo3D6JkQ1JcbLg-JBf2uDw8EBy6BoCeloQAvD_BwE [Accessed 25 November 2024].

Stowell, L., Cox, A., and McKnight, C. (2019). *The American Duchess Guide to 18th Century Beauty: 40 Projects for Period-Accurate Hairstyles, Makeup and Accessories.* Salem, MA: Page Street Publishing.

Stremlau, R. (2011). *Sustaining the Cherokee Family: Kinship and the Allotment of an Indigenous Nation.* Chapel Hill, NC: The University of North Carolina Press.

Tagg, J. (2021). *The Burden of Representation: Essays on Photographies and Histories.* Minneapolis, MN: the University of Minnesota Press.

Talbot, C. (1943). *The Complete Book of Sewing*. New York, NY: Book Presentations.

This Land Press. (2017). *Race Reader: A Literary Chronicle of Conflict and Oppression in the Middle of America*. Tulsa, Oklahoma: This Land Press.

Thomas, H. (2021). Women's Fashion History Through Newspapers: 1900–1920. [Online] Available at: https://blogs.loc.gov/headlinesandheroes/2021/06/womens-fashion-history-through-newspapers-1900–1920/ [Accessed 20 February 2024].

Ulrich, L. (2001). *The Age of Homespun: Objects and Stories in the Creation of an American Myth*. New York, NY: Knopf.

United States Census 1860, Canadian District, Cherokee Nation, Indian Lands, Arkansas; Roll: M653_52; Page: 1187, #391; Family History Library Film: 803052.

United States Commission on Civil Rights. (2021). The U.S. Commission on Civil Rights Marks the 100th Anniversary of the Tulsa Race Massacre. [Online] Available at: https://www.usccr.gov/news/2021/us-commission-civil-rights-marks-100th-anniversary-tulsa-race-massacre [Accessed 28 August 2024].

United States Department of Labor (1929). History of Wages in the United States From Colonial Times to 1928: Bulletin of the United States Bureau of Labor Statistics, No. 499. [Online] Available at: https://fraser.stlouisfed.org/title/history-wages-united-states-colonial-times-1928-4067?start_page=225 [Accessed 1 February 2024].

Ware, T. (2023). *Maryland in the French and Indian War*. Charleston, SC: The History Press.

Weaver, J. (1997). *That the People Might Live: Native American Literatures and Native American Community*. New York, NY: Oxford University Press.

White, P. (2004). "Stand Fast": The Story of Surry Eaton "White Sut" Beck. [Online] Available at: https://gateway.okhistory.org/ark:/67531/metadc2016920/ [Accessed 1 February 2022].

Willett, C. and Cunnington, P. (1992). *The History of Underclothes*. New York, NY: Dover Publications.

Sources of fabric and other material resources

Burnley and Trowbridge https://burnleyandtrowbridge.com/

Redthreaded Corsets https://redthreaded.com/

Sartor Bohemia https://www.sartorbohemia.com/

Victorian Photography Studio https://www.victorianphotostudio.com/

Recommended further reading

Baker, S., Boney, Jr., R., Ganteaume, C. and Tehee, C. (2018). *After Removal: Rebuilding the Cherokee Nation*. Canada: Helmerich Center for American Research at Gilcrease Museum.

Baker, T. and Baker, J. eds. (1996). *The WPA Oklahoma Slave Narratives*. Norman, OK: The University of Oklahoma Press.

Conley, R. (2005). *The Cherokee Nation: A History*. Albuquerque, NM: University of New Mexico Press.

Davis, M. (2015). *No Lady of Leisure: Clothing for the Victorian and Edwardian Working Woman*. https://www.marnajeandavis.com/

Not Your Momma's History http://www.notyourmommashistory.com/

Index

A Map of Tulsa 164

American Board of Commissioners of Foreign Missions 30

American Revolution museum in Washington, D.C. 137

An Address to the Whites Delivered in the First Presbyterian Church 32

Anglo-American culture 29

Anglo-American women 51

anti-racist; American Civil War interpretation community 160; *The American Duchess Guide to 18th Century Beauty* 158–159; Booker T. Washington 162–165; brunch-and-get-dressed party 159; Cheyney McKnight 160; citizen archivist 169; cultural appropriation 158; eighteenth-century-style clothes 159; eighteenth-century-styled sites 160; Facebook 161; "family tree" style websites 166; federal adoption 161; harm and distress 162; historical document scanner 168; historic-style clothes 161

authentic Indian 47

black-and-white photographic image 72

chattel slavery 40

Cherokee culture; adoption of majority cultural norms 29; American cultural memory 44–48; assimilation 28–29; audience participation 28; Cherokee Nation 43–44; cultural Venn diagram 44; depict Polly 79; Euro-American historians 28; Indian Territory 44; more traditionally 27; Native people 28; nineteenth century Cherokee identities (*see* nineteenth century Cherokee identities); Polly's removal story 48; Ruth Margaret Muskrat Bronson 44–48; self-preservation 29; settler colonialism 43; social and historical configurations 42

Cherokee National Council 104

Cherokee Phoenix 62–63, 104

Cherokee women's adoption of European-American; 1835 American census-takers 63; Anglo-American women 51; Cherokee Traditional Dress 49; cotton fabric 64; cultural exchange 52; descriptions of Cherokee people 49; European-style clothes 49; European-style spinning 59–60; European-style textiles 58, 61; spinning wheels 59, 60; twentieth-century Tear Dress 49

Cheyney McKnight; Michael Harriot 174; Pinkster Sew Along of 2024 170

Civil War 6, 9, 12, 16, 17, 43, 68, 81, 83, 85, 87, 112, 117, 150, 160, 165, 182

corset 58, 64, 113–115, 118, 120–124, 126, 137, 151, 153, 156

crinolettes 126

Daniel Heath Justice 31

Davy Crockett 53

Deb Salisbury, The Mantua-Maker Historical Sewing Patterns 152

Dolly Varden outfit 150

dressed Polly; 1830s corded stays 137–139; 1845 work dress 143–147; accessories 129; bodice and outer skirts 152–155; bustle 152; Calico 131–134; chemise 124, 125, 151; chemisette 140, 156; choosing years to depict 117; corded petticoat with lining 135; corset 151; corset cover 126, 127, 152; crinolettes 126; Drawers 119; early 1870s ensemble 147–150; fashion information 105–106; history-themed dress 177; Ivory sateen corset 120, 121; latest fashion 105; layer of clothing 126; Madame Askew 113–114; manuals and advertisements 113; materials 120; nineteenth-century-style underclothes 113; other accessories 156; petticoat bodice 126; petticoats 127, 128; profusion of hat styles 129, 130; red cotton bustle 127, 128; shift 135, 136; skirt supports 126; sleeves 156; small bustle 139; soft corset 120; tucked sateen petticoat with lace flounce 136–137; under-petticoat 135; working-class American women 105

Eastern Cherokee Applications of 1906–1909 13

Elizabeth Stewart Clark (2010) 141

enslaved people 24, 41, 83–86, 88, 98, 166, 174

European-American dress 116

Everyday Fashion in Found Photographs 153

Fairfax County Park Authority 177

George Washington 59

Godey's Lady's Book 106

Henry Laurens Dawes (1816–1903) 18, 19

History of the Cherokee Indians and Their Legends and Folk Lore 24

honoring Polly Beck; Cherokee women 183; Civil War 182; cluster of violence in 1872 182; indigenous women's safety 183; modern discourse 181; *The Personal is Political* 181

Indians are People, Too 45

intellectual warfare 55

intermarriage 24, 31, 34, 35, 42, 73, 85, 104

International Indian Council 56

John Ross 33

legal Cherokees; American Civil War 87; chattel slavery 83; Cherokee Freedmen Project Committee 101; Cherokee leaders in Indian Territory 85; Civil War 81; Dawes Commission's 88–90; publicly acknowledging specific oppressions 90–92; self-conscious awareness 86

Library Company of Philadelphia 57

Lovecraft Country 92

Making Victorian Costumes for Women by Heather Audin 155

Mary Evelyn Rogers 35

National Museum of African American History and Culture in 2019 74

Native American 27, 32, 45, 47, 66–69, 71, 72, 177

nineteenth century Cherokee identities; 1984 analysis, McLoughlin 33; ancestors 30–31; Anglo-Americans 31; antimiscegenation sentiment 37; Bachelors of Cornwall Valley 37; chattel slavery 40; clan-based systems 38; conflating domestic work and civilization 30; cultural adaptation 42; Daniel Heath Justice 35; development of Cherokee civilization 32; Euro-American culture 29, 37; federal agents 34, 40–41; "full-blood" and "mixed-blood" 34–35; gained education and business acumen 36; government-funded and controlled newspaper 33; human communities 33; Intermarriage with White Americans 34; issue of blood quantum 33; legal change 39; Mary Evelyn Rogers 35; non-Indian culture 31; package of "civilization" 40; race-oriented hierarchy 39; Rebecca Nagle 41; slaveholding 41–42; Theda Perdue 29; White American assessment 36, 37

Oklahoma Commission to Study the Tulsa Race Riot of 1921 164

Oklahoma Slave Narratives 93

petticoat bodice 126

photography and self-presentation, Indian territory; Buffalo Bill's Wild West Show 69; chemical process 65; commercial commodities 68; daguerreotypes 66, 67; deculturation and geographic dispossession 72; early photography, discerning color in 72–74; ethnographic veracity, lack of 70; George Eastman 70; Geronimo's Story 69; Jennie Ross Cobb 70; light-sensitive silver iodide 65; Molly Rogers 64; multi-layered project 74; Native Americans 66, 67; oil painting 66; public consumption 68; wet-plate photography 79

Pinkster Sew Along of 2024 170

Rachel Ward; application for enrollment 96; Cherokee citizenship 93; Dawes Commission 92–93; Dawes enrollment packet 94; Freedman enrollment 94; Oklahoma Historical Society 93; testimony 94

Ralph Henry Gabriel 38

sewing machine; changes in industrial production 110; labor-saving devices 111; modern industrial clothing production methods 109; Seamstress 109, 110; techniques 112, 113

skirt supports 126

Sleeping with the Ancestors 173

Smithsonian National Museum of the American Indian's 47

Tarpley, Thompson & Company Store 162

The American Duchess Guide to 18th Century Beauty 158–159

The Cherokee Advocate in 1871 106

The Dressmaker's Guide 117, 118

The Inconvenient Indian 45

The Personal is Political 181

The Workwoman's Guide 140

Trail of Tears 43, 47, 48

Victorian Fashion in America 152

Victorian Photography Studio on the Redthreaded blog 75

Wilma Mankiller 31

Works Progress Administration (WPA) 97

www.ingramcontent.com/pod-product-compliance
Lightning Source LLC
Chambersburg PA
CBHW070804230426
43665CB00017B/2477